THE ROYAL DECCAN HORSE
IN THE GREAT WAR

THE ROYAL DECCAN HORSE IN THE GREAT WAR

BY
LIEUTENANT-COLONEL E. TENNANT
(*Late 20th Deccan Horse*)

The Naval & Military Press Ltd

Reproduced by kind permission of the Central Library,
Royal Military Academy, Sandhurst

Published by
The Naval & Military Press Ltd
Unit 10, Ridgewood Industrial Park,
Uckfield, East Sussex,
TN22 5QE England
Tel: +44 (0) 1825 749494
Fax: +44 (0) 1825 765701
www.naval-military-press.com
www.military-genealogy.com
© The Naval & Military Press Ltd 2008

In reprinting in facsimile from the original, any imperfections are inevitably reproduced and the quality may fall short of modern type and cartographic standards.

Printed and bound by Lightning Source

PREFACE

AFTER a lapse of twenty years it has been no easy task to collect sufficient data from which to compile a record of the deeds of the regiment during the Great War. Many of those who served with it in France and Palestine are no longer with us, and even those few who still remain are diffident about trusting their memories regarding details of the actions in which they took part; so that, if some of the events are more fully described than others, it is not because they are considered as being of more importance, but merely owing to the fact that more information has been available concerning them.

My grateful thanks are due to the Director of the Historical Section (Military Branch) of the Committee of Imperial Defence for placing at my disposal the War Diaries and other documents relating to the regiment; to Mrs. Maclean Coles for her constant and unfailing assistance from the initiation of this work to its completion; to Mr. E. B. Dobson for his great kindness in preparing the maps, in the execution of which he has spared neither time nor trouble; and to Colonel Adams, D.S.O., for his notes on some of the actions in which the regiment was engaged.

In conclusion, the thanks of all members of the regiment—both past and present—are due to Lieutenant-Colonel F. B. N. Tinley, M.C., the present Commandant, for having initiated the idea of a War History, and without whose active support and approval it could never have been carried out.

Lieutenant-Colonel.

EAST HENDRED.

CONTENTS

THE ROYAL DECCAN HORSE

	PAGE
FOREWORD BY BRIGADIER-GENERAL C. E. MACQUOID, C.I.E., D.S.O., COLONEL, THE ROYAL DECCAN HORSE	xiii

CHAP.

I. 1816 TO 1914 1
Early History—Successive Titles borne by the Regiment—Incorporation with Regular Army—High Standard of Efficiency—Composition and Personnel.

II. AUGUST 1914 TO NOVEMBER 1914 7
Mobilization—H.E.H. The Nizam of Hyderabad—Formation of Depot—Embarkation at Bombay—Voyage to Europe—Marseilles—Orléans—Vieille Chapelle.

III. 1ST NOVEMBER 1914 TO 19TH DECEMBER 1914 16
Sector of Front assigned to Indian Army Corps—First Experience of Active Service—Béthune—Inspections by H.R.H. The Prince of Wales and H.R.H. Prince Arthur of Connaught—Trench Warfare—Special Order of the Day by H.M. King George V—Christmas, 1914—Description of Country and Trenches—Shortage of Shells.

IV. 19TH DECEMBER 1914 TO 31ST DECEMBER 1914 24
German Capture of Trenches at Festubert—Despatch of Secunderabad Cavalry Brigade as Reinforcements—Givenchy—Casualties—Gallantry of Captain Ross and Lieutenant Tinley—Formation of 2nd Indian Cavalry Division—Farewell Letter from General Willcocks.

V. 1915 34
Inspections—Neuve Chapelle—Belgian Frontier—Visit of T.M. The King and Queen of the Belgians—Loos—Departure of Indian Infantry for Mesopotamia.

VI. 1916 44
Cavalry Reorganization—St. Riquier—Somme Valley—Delville Wood—Formation of Cavalry Corps—Pioneer Companies.

VII. 1917 53
German Retirement—Trefcon—Raids by Second-Lieutenant Godfree and Captain Mulloy—Vadencourt Sector—Concentration for Passchendaele—Belgian Frontier—Cambrai—Gouzeaucourt.

VIII. 1ST JANUARY 1918 TO 15TH AUGUST 1918 62
Indian Cavalry ordered to Palestine—Embarkation at Marseilles—Arrival at Alexandria—Advance to Belah—Formation of 14th Cavalry Brigade and 5th Cavalry Division—Situation in Palestine—Desert Mounted Corps—Jordan Valley—Issue of Lances—El Ghoraniye.

CHAP.		PAGE
IX.	15TH AUGUST 1918 TO 30TH SEPTEMBER 1918	71
	Plan for General Advance—Description of Country—Concentration of Mounted Troops—The Advance—Carmel Range—Afule—Athlit—March to Damascus—Kiswe—Ashrafie—Fall of Damascus.	
X.	1ST OCTOBER 1918 TO 31ST DECEMBER 1918	82
	Advance to Homs—Lure of Aleppo—Advance of 5th Cavalry Division from Homs—Fall of Aleppo—Armistice—Record of 5th Cavalry Division—Lessons from the Campaign.	
XI.	1919 TO 1921	89
	Rioting in Aleppo—Break up of Desert Mounted Corps—Formation of North Force—Beirut—Embarkation for Egypt—Kantara—Farewell Message from Lord Allenby—Return to India—Award to the Regiment of title " Royal "—Grant of Battle Honours—Amalgamation with 29th Lancers (Deccan Horse).	

29TH LANCERS (DECCAN HORSE)

FOREWORD BY BRIGADIER-GENERAL W. J. LAMBERT, D.S.O., LAST COMMANDANT OF THE 29TH LANCERS (DECCAN HORSE)	113
INTRODUCTORY NOTE	121
29TH LANCERS, 1914-1920	123

APPENDICES

THE ROYAL DECCAN HORSE

APPENDIX		PAGE
A.	LIST OF AWARDS RECEIVED	94
B.	BRITISH OFFICERS WHO SERVED WITH THE REGIMENT IN THE FIELD DURING THE GREAT WAR	97
C.	ROLL OF OFFICERS AND MEN WHO LOST THEIR LIVES IN THE GREAT WAR	99
D.	THE SILLADAR SYSTEM	101
E.	CAVALRY IN MODERN WAR	106
F.	COMMANDANTS OF THE REGIMENT FROM THE YEAR 1818	110

29TH LANCERS (DECCAN HORSE)

A.	HONOURS AND AWARDS	175
B.	BRITISH OFFICERS WHO SERVED ON ACTIVE SERVICE WITH THE 29TH LANCERS	178
C.	OFFICERS, NON-COMMISSIONED OFFICERS AND MEN WHO LOST THEIR LIVES IN THE GREAT WAR	180

LIST OF PLATES

TRUMPET BANNER, THE ROYAL DECCAN HORSE ... ... *Frontispiece*

                                                                                     FACING PAGE

RISSALDAR (DECCAN MUHAMMADAN), XXTH DECCAN HORSE, 1914 4

HYDERABAD CONTINGENT CAVALRY ("REFORMED HORSE"), 1845 114

LIST OF MAPS

                                                                                                       FACING PAGE

GIVENCHY 32

DELVILLE WOOD 52

PALESTINE, 1ST PHASE 78

PALESTINE, 2ND PHASE 88

FRANCE, 1914–1918 182

FOREWORD

BY

BRIGADIER-GENERAL C. E. MACQUOID, C.I.E., D.S.O.
Colonel, The Royal Deccan Horse

HAVING been invited by Lieutenant-Colonel Tinley, the present Commandant, to write a Foreword to this War History of the Regiment, I do not think I can do better than give a very brief account of those fine old soldiers, the Deccan Muhammadan, the Deccan Rajput and the Deccan Sikh, who were still to be found in its ranks on the outbreak of the War. For the data I am almost entirely indebted to Gribble's *History of the Deccan*, Vol. I, which I can confidently recommend to anyone interested in the history of that particular part of the Indian Empire over which H.E.H. the Nizam of Hyderabad holds sway.

The Deccan Muhammadan.—In 1294 Ala-ud-din, nephew and son-in-law of Jellal-ud-din, Sultan of Delhi, having secretly collected an army, disappeared, and, except for vague rumours which filtered through to Delhi that he was fighting Hindoos at Deogiri, later better known as Dowlatabad, nothing whatever was heard of his plans or movements. Then suddenly Ala-ud-din returned to Bengal, accompanied only by an escort plus a huge treasure "so great that it was said nothing like it had ever been seen before." Attracted by rumours of the immense wealth to be found in the Deccan there commenced numerous Muhammadan invasions from the north. The leaders of these invasions waged constant war with each other in the Deccan and carved out for themselves various Sultanates, of which the principal were Ahmednagar, Golcondah, Bijapur and, still further to the south, Vijayanagar. The descendants of these first invaders became known as, and styled themselves, " Deccan " Muhammadans, in distinction to invaders of a later date who were " Mogul " Muhammadans.

The Deccan Rajput.—However, the Muhammadans of 1294 were not the first to discover the wealth of the Deccan, for on their arrival they found that a great part of the hilly country, constituting the northern boundary of the Deccan, was already in the possession of various Rajput princes. These Rajput princes disputed the possession of the land, and in consequence continuous warfare ensued between these two races. Eventually peace was established and those Rajputs who permanently settled in the Deccan became known as " Deccan " Rajputs.

The Deccan Sikh.—At the commencement of the eighteenth century Guru Govind Singh, the tenth and last Guru of the Sikhs, who was held in the highest esteem by the Sikh nation, not only on account of his religious principles but also for his soldierly qualities, received an invitation from the Mogul Emperor, Bahadur Shah (eldest son of Aurungzebe) to visit him at his court. Govind Singh accepted and was treated with the greatest respect and honour by the Emperor, who offered him a high military command at Nander, on the banks of the Godavery in the Deccan. This was accepted, and towards the end of 1703 Govind Singh took up his headquarters at that town. Here, in 1708, he was assassinated by a Pathan in revenge for the death of his grandfather, who had met his death at the hands of the Guru. In the course of time a shrine was erected at Nander to the memory of Guru Govind Singh and to this shrine there came pilgrimages of Sikhs to worship and pay homage. Many of these Sikhs remained in the Deccan and took up service under the Nizam and his nobles, and their descendants were known as Deccan Sikhs.

In the later part of the seventeenth century there commenced another series of invasions on the part of the " Mogul "

Emperors reigning at Delhi. In order to repel these the Muhammadan rulers of the Deccan Sultanates formed an alliance and enlisted the Deccan Rajputs in their armies to swell their ranks, and thus commenced those amicable relations which henceforth existed between the Deccan Muhammadans and the Deccan Rajputs. The last, the best-known and the greatest of these Mogul invasions was that led by the Emperor Aurungzebe in person. For close on sixty years (1650 to 1707) Aurungzebe waged war, first against the Deccan Sultans and then against the Mahrattas, and eventually formed a united kingdom of the Deccan under his own personal rule. He died at the age of ninety and was buried at Aurungabad, which he had made his capital and which was named after him. Chief amongst Aurungzebe's men was one Chin Kulich Khan, a military leader of note and sagacious in council, who held many high appointments with credit to himself and his master. After Aurungzebe's death Chin Kulich Khan was confirmed in his appointments by the Emperor's successor and subsequently promoted to be Subadar of the Deccan, with the title of Asaf Jah, Nizam-ul-Mulk. A point of especial interest to the regiment is the fact that our Honorary Colonel, "Honorary Lieutenant-General 'His Exalted Highness' Asaf Jah, Muzzaffar-ul-Mulk, Wal Mumalik, Nizam-ud-Daula, Nawab Sir Mir Usman Ali Khan Bahadur, Fateh Jung, Faithful Ally of the British Government, G.C.S.I., G.B.E., Nizam of Hyderabad and Berar," is the direct descendant of the above-named Chin Kulich Khan, first Nizam of Hyderabad, who died in 1748, over one hundred years of age, after breaking away from the sovereignty of the Mogul Emperor at Delhi and establishing a separate and independent kingdom of the Deccan.

For three and a half centuries the Deccan Muhammadans and Deccan Rajputs had been engaged in unceasing warfare to be followed by another century and a half of strife against the Mahrattas. It will thus be seen that for generations they had been soldiers born and bred, than which there were none better in those days, and all the tactics, stratagems and tricks of war which were employed by the Mahrattas, under their great chieftain Sivajee, were those learnt from their foes in the Deccan.

After the Indian Mutiny the regiment was not called upon to take part in any major campaign until the Great War, so that during this long interval of peace the Deccan soldier turned to other occupations, and the right stamp of men commenced to decline. Nevertheless, in 1914 there were still in the regiment two squadrons composed of Deccan Muhammadans and Deccan Rajputs, and in no way did they fail in acting up to the traditions of their ancestors. They, equally with the Sikhs and Jats, contributed towards the highest honour a regiment can obtain, for after the conclusion of the War, by favour of His Majesty the King and Emperor of India, it was accorded the great distinction of the prefix " Royal " to its title. The remaining portion of the title, viz. : " Deccan Horse," helps to maintain the link with the land for which the ancestors of the regiment struggled and conquered.

Towards the end of the eighteenth century the British, from Madras, were fringeing upon the southern boundary of the Deccan, and in the course of time there followed an alliance between the East India Company and the Nizam, which developed later in the formation of the Hyderabad Contingent. The history of this Corps, from its creation in 1800 up to the time when it was transferred from the control of the Governor-General to that of the Commander-in-Chief in India, will be found fully set out in Major R. G. Burton's *History of the Hyderabad Contingent*. Every Officer should read this work for, apart from matters of general interest, Major Burton gives much information regarding the political situation in the Deccan at the commencement of the nineteenth century, which is not easily available to the general reader.

The thanks of the regiment that its history has been brought up to date are due in the first place to Lieutenant-Colonel Tinley, the Commandant, who had the initiative to get it started, and especially to Lieutenant-Colonel Tennant, its historian, who, I know, has spared no pains or trouble to make it as accurate as possible.

My father was appointed to the Hyderabad Contingent from the old Madras Army in 1852 and died on his way home to England on retirement. I was appointed to the Hyderabad Contingent from my British regiment as a boy of eighteen years of age, in 1888, but had to bide my time till a vacancy occurred in the cavalry. I was exceptionally honoured in being made Colonel of the regiment, which distinction I resign this year on attaining the age of seventy years, when, through my father, my long connection of eighty-six years with the regiment ceases.

It only remains for me to send my kind remembrances to all old soldiers who may read this History and may bear me in mind. To the present and future Officers and men in the regiment, I wish all success in their "comings and goings," of whatsoever nature they may be, and "God-speed."

C. E. Macquoid

Brigadier-General,
Colonel, The Royal Deccan Horse.

THE ROYAL DECCAN HORSE

THE ROYAL DECCAN HORSE

CHAPTER I

1816 TO 1914

Early History—Successive Titles borne by the Regiment—Incorporation with Regular Army—High Standard of Efficiency—Composition and Personnel.

BEFORE commencing a record of the services of The Royal Deccan Horse in the Great War, it will not be out of place to give a brief sketch of the early history of the regiment prior to its being honoured with its present title of "Royal," for it has borne no fewer than six designations since it was first raised in 1816.*

In the year 1790, as the result of a treaty of offensive and defensive alliance between the Honourable East India Company and the Nizam of Hyderabad, the latter undertook to raise and maintain a body of 10,000 cavalry—many of whom served in the Seringapatam Campaign in 1799—the cost of which was to be defrayed by the East India Company. This body of cavalry consisted of levies raised by the various chieftains of Berar, but in the year 1816 it was reorganized and became "The Reformed Horse," composed of four regiments, under the command of British Officers of the East India Company's army. The 1st (or, Nawab Jalal-ud-Daula) Regiment was commanded by Captains Davies and Clerk.

In 1826 a further reorganization took place and the "Nawab-ud-Daula" Regiment became the 1st Regiment, Nizam's Cavalry. By the terms of the treaty, the Nizam's mounted troops (whether

* A fuller record will be found in Major R. G. Burton's *History of the Hyderabad Contingent*, from which most of the information in this summary has been obtained.

known as Reformed Horse, Nizam's Cavalry, or later, as the Hyderabad Contingent) had to be permanently quartered within the boundaries of the Nizam's dominions, and it is probably on this account that, in later years, the idea became prevalent in some quarters that it was a force which merely lazed away its time in quiet cantonments. This was by no means the case, and it is very much to be doubted whether any regiments of the Indian Army can show such a record of continuous active service. In 1817, within a year of its reorganization as the Reformed Horse, the regiment was employed in a great war, known as the Pindari and Maratha War, which involved almost the whole of Central India. At the investment and capture of Mahidpur, Nagpur, and Nowah, the Reformed Horse earned for themselves an imperishable name. That their efficiency continued to be maintained at the highest pitch is evidenced by a statement made in 1853 by Lord Gough—the Commander-in-Chief in India—before a House of Commons Committee, in which he described the Nizam's Cavalry as being "the first irregular cavalry in the world."

In 1854, when a further reorganization took place, the regiment was re-named the 1st Cavalry, Hyderabad Contingent.

"For forty years" (prior to 1856) "they (the Hyderabad Contingent) had been engaged in continuous fighting, and scarcely a month had passed without some portion of the Force being on active service in the field, so that, in fact, they may be said to have been a field force from the very commencement. They passed as much time on active service as they did in their small and isolated cantonments, and their training was consequently such as to fit them best for undertaking their rôle in a larger theatre of war."*

On the outbreak of the Indian Mutiny, the Hyderabad Contingent not only remained true to its salt, but, by its attitude

* Burton's *History of the Hyderabad Contingent*, p. 142.

and its deeds, saved the situation in Southern India. Later, when the force took the field in Central India, it earned for itself a great reputation by deeds which are unsurpassed by those of any of our Indian troops.

In his Despatch after the action at Banda in 1858, General Whitlock wrote :—

" It is a pleasant duty to bring to the special notice of His Excellency the Commander-in-Chief, the name of Captain Macintyre, commanding a squadron of the 2nd Hyderabad Contingent Cavalry, always distinguished for his zeal, a soldier's spirit and a judgment well fitting him for his command; his charge on the enemy's guns was the admiration of all who witnessed the affair and his men followed their leader with an ardour with which his high bearing inspired them and I cannot express myself in too high terms of their spirit and gallantry."

It was not without cause that Sir Hugh Rose, after they had marched a thousand miles with him and distinguished themselves in many actions, called the Hyderabad Contingent cavalry " the wings of the army."

The Hyderabad Contingent was also employed in the Second Afghan War of 1879-80, the Burmah War of 1886-88, and in China in 1900. But apart from these major wars, some portion of the Hyderabad Contingent was engaged on active service, of one kind or another, for three years out of every four, from the date of its inception right up to 1903, when it was incorporated with the regular Indian Army.

In the early days the Nizam's territories were constantly raided by hordes of Pindaris, Bhils, Rohillas and other marauding tribes from the outside, as well as being harried from within by strong bands of dacoits. These latter continued to give trouble right up to the year 1899, when Captain Humfrey and Lieutenant Fagan, with a squadron of the regiment, attacked a large gang of dacoits near Bir, of whom they killed ten, wounded sixteen and brought back thirty-eight prisoners.

In 1890, the title of the regiment was changed from "1st Cavalry, Hyderabad Contingent" to "1st Lancers, Hyderabad Contingent."

In 1903, owing to a fresh agreement having been made with the Nizam's Government, the Hyderabad Contingent ceased to be a localized force and became incorporated with the regular Indian Army; the title of the regiment being once more changed from "1st Lancers, Hyderabad Contingent" to "The XXth Deccan Horse," under which designation it served throughout the Great War. One effect of this change was to put an end to a feeling of isolation which had begun to grow up in the Contingent. Through being a strictly localized force and not borne on the strength of any of the old Presidency armies of Bengal, Bombay, and Madras, the merits of both officers and men serving in the Hyderabad Contingent were apt to be overlooked, more especially in the case of appointments to the higher commands. Lord Gough's opinion in 1853 has already been quoted, and that this high standard continued to be maintained is borne out by the report of an Inspector-General of Cavalry in more recent times, from which the following is an extract:—

"I have always heard the Hyderabad Contingent Cavalry well spoken of, so that on coming here I was prepared to see something good, but I must cordially say that what I have seen of your regiment has greatly exceeded anything I expected. During my inspection I have found the same efficiency throughout and I can only say that if ever it should be my fortune to command cavalry on service I should not wish to have a finer regiment with me."

Before concluding this brief summary it may be of interest to add a few words regarding the composition of the Hyderabad Contingent Cavalry. Prior to 1854 each regiment consisted of

RISSALDAR (DECCAN MUHAMMADAN)
XXth DECCAN HORSE
1914

four squadrons, but in that year the number was reduced to three (solely in order to reduce expense) and this establishment was maintained until 1903, when the number of squadrons was again increased to four per regiment, one squadron being sent from the 3rd Lancers to each of the three remaining regiments.

Personnel

In 1816, when Captain Davies assumed charge, he found the men to be of the best description, mostly Muhammadans from the North of Hindustan, mixed with a few foreigners from Baluchistan and Sind. In November of the same year the strength was increased by a reinforcement of fifteen hundred men from Hyderabad, consisting, for the most part, of Pathans and Moguls. The descendants of all these mixed races became classified later as Deccan Muhammadans.

The Muhammadans long remained the nucleus of the cavalry, but gradually Sikhs and Jats were introduced and the class squadron system was adopted in each regiment in 1895.

Until 1880 there were never more than three British Officers in each regiment, but in that year the number was raised to four. In 1888 the number was increased to six, and in 1892 to eight per regiment. Subsequently the regiment was maintained on the same footing as the Bengal Cavalry as regards the strength of British Officers.

A paucity of British Officers has this advantage—that it throws more work, responsibility, and independence, upon the Indian Officers, thus increasing their efficiency, which is liable to deteriorate when everything is done by the British Officers. Perhaps it is to this that the extraordinary efficiency of the Hyderabad Contingent Cavalry in the early days is mainly to be ascribed.

In addition to having afforded frequent opportunities for junior officers to gain experience of active-service conditions, the territory included in H.E.H. The Nizam's dominions provides the finest training area for cavalry in the whole of India, and the late Field-Marshal Earl Haig, when Inspector-General of Cavalry in India, selected Hyderabad, Deccan, as being the most suitable locality for one of his big cavalry staff rides.

On the 20th November 1907 the XXth Deccan Horse left the Deccan and marched to Bangalore, where it remained, as part of the garrison, until the 15th October 1912, when it returned to Bolarum, and then, together with "N" Battery, Royal Horse Artillery, the 7th Dragoon Guards, and the 34th Poona Horse, formed the 9th (Secunderabad) Cavalry Brigade, under the command of Brigadier-General F. Wadeson.

The composition of the regiment at the time of the outbreak of the war was as follows:—

Commandant	Lieutenant-Colonel G. E. D. Elsmie.
Second-in-Command	Lieutenant-Colonel F. W. C. Turner (leave, England).
Adjutant	Captain C. D. Gregson.
Quartermaster	Captain C. F. Clarke.
Woordie-Major	Jemadar Mahbub Khan II.
Medical Officer	Lieutenant-Colonel Fleming, I.M.S.

"A" *Squadron* (*Sikhs*).
Major E. Tennant.
Captain Jarvis (Commandant, Madras Body Guard).
Lieutenant Dickinson (sick leave, England).
Rissaldar-Major Jhermal Singh.
Ressaidar Prem Singh.
Jemadar Mangal Singh.
Jemadar Kishan Singh.

"B" *Squadron* (*Jats*).
Major F. Adams (leave, England).
Captain R. B. Worgan (leave, England) (Commandant, Bengal Body Guard).
Captain A. E. H. Ley.
Rissaldar Nigahia Ram.
Ressaidar Brij Lal.
Jemadar Dalip Singh I.
Jemadar Ramji Lal.

"C" *Squadron* (*Deccan Muhammadans*).
Captain J. S. McEuen (leave, England).
Captain C. C. Mackenzie (Personal Assistant to Resident, Mysore).
Lieutenant F. Oswald (sick leave, England).
Lieutenant F. B. N. Tinley.
Rissaldar Mir Hadayat Ali.
Rissaldar Abdul Ghani Khan.
Jemadar Mahbub Khan I.
Jemadar Hyat Mir Khan.

"D" *Squadron* (*two Troops Deccan Muhammadans, two Troops Rajputs*).
Captain A. C. Ross.
Lieutenant T. K. Wilson.
Rissaldar Amir Mohammed Khan.
Ressaidar Bachant Singh.
Jemadar Konsal Singh.
Jemadar Mir Sadik Ali.

CHAPTER II

AUGUST 1914 TO NOVEMBER 1914

Mobilization—H.E.H. The Nizam of Hyderabad—Formation of Depot—Embarkation at Bombay—Voyage to Europe—Marseilles—Orléans—Vieille Chapelle.

ON the conclusion of the Field Training season in the spring of 1914, there being neither wars nor rumours of wars, the regiment settled down to the usual hot-weather routine. Towards the end of July speculation became rife as to whether there would be a war in Europe, but the consensus of opinion was that the crisis would blow over. Excitement rose, however, when England declared war on Germany on the 4th August, but even then there appeared to be small likelihood of the services of the Indian Army being required, at any rate for the present. Then suddenly, on the evening of the 9th August, telegraphic orders were received for the Brigade to mobilize for service out of India. Being "Silladar," the regiment was responsible for providing everything—horses, transport, tents, saddlery, clothing, equipment (rifles, revolvers, ammunition and signalling equipment excepted). Nothing could be drawn from Government arsenals or supply departments. Thanks, however, to the high state of efficiency in which the regiment was habitually maintained, no replacements were found necessary and mobilization proceeded without a hitch, in spite of the fact that there were only five British Officers (excluding the Commanding Officer, Adjutant, Quartermaster and Medical Officer) present with the regiment during the whole of this period, including embarkation.

Since the orders specified that the regiment was to proceed at full strength, drafts of both men and horses had to be obtained from the linked regiment (33rd Light Cavalry) in order to make good shortages due to recruits not yet sufficiently trained for active service and remounts still in the riding-school. For this purpose a draft of one Indian Officer and forty-three rank and file was received from the 33rd Light Cavalry.

Under the regulations in force at the time, British Officers of the Indian cavalry had to provide themselves with chargers at their own expense and, as must necessarily happen, some of these, being still under training in the riding-school or temporarily incapacitated through minor injuries, were unfit for immediate active service. In order to make good the deficiencies, trained chargers were essential, but from where could such be obtained? Owing to war having been declared, and the news broadcast over the country that Indian cavalry were being sent to France, not a single officer in any regiment, even though not yet mobilized, was willing to sell a trained charger, and no other source was apparently available. At this juncture H.E.H. The Nizam of Hyderabad (Honorary Colonel of the regiment) the " Faithful Ally of the British Government," came to the regiment's assistance and issued instructions to Lieutenant-Colonel Sir Afsur ul Mulk, K.C.I.E., the Commander-in-Chief of the Hyderabad Imperial Service Troops, to send up a batch of well-trained chargers from which those officers short of horses made good their deficiencies. In addition, he supplied every officer and man present with the regiment with a pair of cord breeches.

Only a few months previously, His Exalted Highness had shown his interest in the regiment by undertaking to defray the entire cost of rearming all ranks with the new-pattern cavalry thrusting sword, and this order had been placed with Messrs. Wilkinson & Co., of Pall Mall, who delivered the swords in France in the following spring. The pattern—especially designed for the regiment—was so highly approved of that it has since been adopted as the regulation sword for all Indian cavalry. The generosity of His Exalted Highness and his active interest in the regiment did not end here, for he undertook to defray the entire cost of the regiment whilst on active service and thus relieve the Indian Government of this charge.

Here it may be mentioned that, up to the conclusion of the Great War, all the Indian cavalry (with the exception of the three regiments of Madras cavalry) were maintained on the Silladar System (a short description of which is given in Appendix D, p. 101), but the system was abolished upon the return of the regiment to India. Whether it would not have been wiser, both on the score of economy, popularity and the fostering of a spirit of self-reliance, to have amended the Silladar System instead of abolishing it altogether, must always remain a debatable subject.

During the period of mobilization an outbreak of cholera occurred in some of the villages close to Bolarum and on the 23rd August two cases were reported in the regiment, one of which proved fatal. Orders were immediately issued to vacate cantonments and move into camp, well away from the infected area; and thanks to the measures carried out on the advice of the medical officer, no further cases occurred and the regiment obtained a clean bill of health.

In order to take charge of the recruits, remounts under training, transport mules, Quartermaster's stores, etc., all of which had to be left behind, a regimental Depot was formed and placed under the command of Captain A. E. H. Ley, with Lieutenant T. K. Wilson, Ressaidar Bachant Singh and Jemadar Sardara Singh as his assistants. This Depot moved to Neemuch on the 14th November 1914 and remained there until the regiment returned from the war and rejoined it on the 17th April 1920.

On the 26th August Major-General Sir R. Phayre, K.C.B., commanding the Secunderabad Division, inspected the regiment and complimented it on its fine appearance, but it was not until the 5th September that it left camp at Bolarum and marched to Secunderabad, escorted by the bands of the infantry regiments of the garrison, for entrainment for Bombay.

The actual strength which left Bolarum was : 9 British Officers (including the Medical Officer), 18 Indian Officers, 540 rank and file, 579 horses. (These figures include the draft of 1 Indian Officer and 43 rank and file received from the 33rd Light Cavalry.)

On arrival at Bombay on the morning of the 7th September the regiment went into camp on the Maidan, behind the Marine Lines, the horses being picketed in the open. The monsoon being practically over, a period of fine weather was anticipated, but unfortunately on the very next day, the 8th, heavy rain fell and continued to do so for several days without a break. As the men were only equipped with light bivouac tents some three and a half feet high and only just big enough for two persons to lie down in, the kits, blankets and saddles were soaked and the horses, being out in the open, without cover, began to lose condition. As the weather showed no sign of improving, a move was made on the 12th to the goods sheds of the B.B. & C.I. Railway Company, and here both men and horses found ample accommodation, and the next few days were spent in drying kits and blankets and in cleaning saddlery and equipment.

On the 15th September the regiment embarked on the s.s. *Egra* and s.s. *Ellora* of the British India Line. It is a coincidence that the s.s. *Ellora* also conveyed the regiment from Bombay to Karachi (on their move from Poona to Quetta) in 1936, so that Lieutenant-Colonel Tinley, M.C., who had first travelled on it as junior subaltern, once more travelled on it as Commandant, twenty-two years later. Owing to information having been received that the German cruiser *Konigsberg* was lying in wait somewhere in the Indian Ocean, departure had to be postponed until a sufficiently strong escort could be provided to protect the convoy. Consequently it was not until the morning of the 20th September that the *Egra* and *Ellora* left Bombay in company with thirty-one other transports (carrying the remainder of the Secunderabad Cavalry Brigade and the major portion of the Meerut Division), under the escort of H.M.S. *Swiftsure*, *Fox* and *Dartmouth*. Four days later the convoy was augmented by the arrival of ten more transports and one cruiser from Karachi, but three transports escorted by one cruiser left (presumably for British East Africa), leaving a total of ships with the main convoy of: H.M.S. *Swiftsure*, two R.I.M. cruisers, forty transports. As the speed of the convoy had to be maintained at that of the slowest ship, progress was not rapid, but the weather being fine and the sea smooth both men and horses quickly settled down and this portion of the voyage was a most enjoyable one. The outlook from deck presented a unique and never-to-be-forgotten sight, for on all sides, right up to the horizon, the ocean appeared to be crowded with ships, all steaming in the same direction and maintaining a steady pace.

Coir matting was laid down over the upper decks and the horses were brought up in batches daily for exercise, whilst the standings were cleaned. Aden was passed on the 28th and from there the escort duty was taken over by H.M.S. *Black Prince*, the *Swiftsure* and R.I.M. cruisers returning to Bombay. The heat in the Red Sea was very trying to the horses below decks and two or three died from heat apoplexy, but otherwise the health of both men and horses remained excellent. It was not until the 3rd October that the convoy arrived at Port Said, where the following officers rejoined from leave in England: Lieutenant-Colonel F. W. C. Turner, Captains J. S. McEuen and R. B. Worgan, and Lieutenant W. Dickinson (who was subsequently thrown from his horse at La Penne camp, Marseilles, and evacuated sick. He never rejoined the regiment).

During the halt at Port Said courtesy visits were paid to the French warships *Jaureguiberry* and *Bouvet* anchored in the roadstead (the latter was lost with all hands some months later in the Dardanelles); and on the 6th the Secunderabad Cavalry Brigade continued the voyage to Marseilles, escorted by the French battleship *Jaureguiberry*. This portion of the voyage was somewhat unpleasant owing to a cold head wind and rough seas, and three horses died from pneumonia. On the 12th October, exactly four weeks after the men and horses had embarked, the convoy arrived safely at Marseilles and the regiment disembarked shortly after noon.

Before leaving the docks all the rifles were exchanged for new ones of the latest pattern. This change was necessary owing to an alteration having been made in the shape of the clip loaders. The strength of the regiment was now augmented by the attachment of two officers, Second-Lieutenants Heaton-Armstrong and H. L. Sunderland (the former eventually became a regular officer of the regiment), and three French non-commissioned officers, to act as interpreters.

At about 3 p.m. the Brigade left the docks and marched on foot, leading the horses, to a camp at La Penne, a distance of about ten miles. It was a bright, sunny day and the welcome afforded by the citizens of Marseilles was most cordial, the streets being packed with cheering crowds. On arrival at La Penne, the camp was speedily marked out, bivouac tents erected and horses pegged down; and by nightfall everything was ship-shape.

Unfortunately, on the following day the weather changed, a chilly mistral started blowing, accompanied by continuous rain, and the camp, being on clay soil, soon became a quagmire and the horse-lines a sea of mud. Conditions became so bad that on the 19th the whole Brigade moved to another and drier camping-ground near the village of Marcel, but hardly had the change been completed than orders were received to strike camp and entrain for the front. The regiment marched from Marcel at 4.30 p.m. on the 20th September to the dock railway station at Arrênes, and at seven o'clock on the morning of the 21st left for Orléans via Cette, Narbonne and Toulouse. At each stopping-place cheering crowds thronged the railway platforms, and gifts of cigarettes, flowers, and picture postcards were showered upon the men, in return for which there was a never-ending demand for souvenirs in the shape of regimental badges, buttons, etc.

Orléans was reached on the morning of the 23rd, but owing to an insufficiency of wheeled transport, the move to camp at La Source (distant about seven miles) was greatly delayed and it was past 11 p.m. before the regiment was complete and settled down. On this day Major F. Adams rejoined the regiment from leave in England and resumed command of " B " Squadron. The situation of the camp at La Source left nothing to be desired and there was ample space for the entire Brigade, both for exercise and drill. The period the regiment spent here was invaluable for getting the horses into condition after their long voyage from India and the cold and wet weather experienced at Marseilles.

Up till now no one had ever contemplated the possibility of cavalry being utilized in any other way than as cavalry, and it came as a shock and a surprise when an issue of infantry bayonets was made to the Brigade. As neither officers nor men had ever received any instruction in the use of the bayonet, and as there was no convenient way of carrying it when mounted, this new weapon was looked upon as somewhat of an encumbrance. What was specially unfortunate was that this particular pattern of bayonet did not fit the new rifles which had been issued to the Brigade on landing at Marseilles and, as will be noticed later on, this had lamentable consequences.

On the 29th October orders were received for the Brigade to move to the front, leaving behind all tents and a ten per cent. reinforcement of both men and horses.

Owing to the necessity for utilizing branch lines well away from the fighting zone, the rail journey from Orléans was slow and tedious, and it was not until the early hours of the 1st November that the regiment arrived at Merville, where it detrained and then marched to billets in the small village of Vieille Chapelle, some two or three miles behind the front line. Up to this time the men had seen none of the effects of modern warfare upon a peaceful countryside, but during the march to Vieille Chapelle their eyes were opened. " The roads and lanes were crowded with terrified civilian refugees fleeing from their homes, despair depicted on their faces. Old people and young women with children, trudging along with huge bundles on their backs, and pushing vehicles of every description—farm carts, hand carts, wheelbarrows and perambulators—loaded to their utmost capacity with the family possessions. Here and there broken vehicles had been abandoned by the side of the road—the contents scattered about and the owners gone. There they remained at the mercy of wind and weather, as there was no means of salving them. The walls of the houses passed were pierced with shell holes, and here and there great craters had been made in the main road and adjacent fields where high-explosive shells had fallen."*

On arrival at Vieille Chapelle, owing to the majority of the inhabitants having left, there was plenty of suitable accommodation both for men and horses, the latter being picketed in the adjacent meadows. In spite of its nearness to the front line, the village had been comparatively unmolested and a few old men and women were still to be seen working in the fields, undaunted by the occasional explosion of shells in their vicinity and determined

* *War History of the Poona Horse.*

to harvest what they could before the arrival of the hated "Boches." Occasionally German scouting planes passed overhead, and the locality was infested with spies, who doubtless found little difficulty in passing information back through the weakly held British line.

The regiment remained at Vieille Chapelle for just a week, and most of this period was occupied in furnishing digging parties to improve and extend the third-line system of trenches in the neighbourhood of Rouge Croix. This was a new experience for all ranks as trench-digging had not hitherto been included in the curriculum of peace training, but everyone set to with a will and, aided by the instruction afforded by the "Sapper" staff in charge, very soon became expert in the work of making trenches.

CHAPTER III*

1st November 1914 to 19th December 1914

Sector of Front assigned to Indian Army Corps—First Experience of Active Service—Béthune—Inspections by H.R.H. The Prince of Wales and H.R.H. Prince Arthur of Connaught—Trench Warfare—Special Order of the Day by H.M. King George V—Christmas, 1914—Description of Country and Trenches—Shortage of Shells.

THE front assigned to the Indian Army Corps, under the command of Lieutenant-General Sir James Willcocks, was about eight miles in length and extended from the village of Givenchy on the right through Le Plantin and Richebourg l'Avoué, past Neuve Chapelle to just north of Mauquissart, the southern half being held by the Meerut Division and the northern by the Lahore Division.

The actual fighting strength of the entire Corps amounted to only a little over 13,000 rifles (of whom 9,500 were Indians); so that it only slightly exceeded the strength of one British Division. In order to hold this long front every unit was required in the fighting line, and up to the time of the arrival of the Secunderabad Cavalry Brigade on 1st November (which at the most might mean 900 rifles) the Corps Commander had absolutely no reserve in his hands. Consequently, as soon as the Brigade reached the front it became a mobile Corps Reserve under the direct orders of the General Officer Commanding.

The German strength directly opposite the Corps may be taken at about 20,000 infantry, in addition to pioneers, and an unknown number of guns of all calibres.

* Most of the subject matter of this chapter has been obtained from General Willcocks' book, *With the Indians in France*.

The distance between the opposing front-line trenches varied from as little as twenty up to eighty yards, so that it was fatal for anyone to expose his head above the parapet during daylight.

Some heavy fighting took place about this time in the sector held by the Lahore Division, and on the 8th November the regiment received orders to hand over all horses to the care of the Jodhpur Lancers (which regiment had been attached to the Brigade at Orléans) and to proceed on foot—as strong as possible—to Pont du Hem and there to report for orders to the G.O.C. 7th Infantry Brigade. By the time the regiment arrived at Pont du Hem matters had quieted down somewhat, so that for the moment its services were not required. In order, however, to be quickly available in case of necessity, it was directed to go into temporary billets in the vicinity of Rouge Croix and to remain there in a state of constant readiness; and here the regiment received its first experience of modern heavy artillery fire and suffered its first casualties.

The Germans had an annoying habit of bombarding this locality for a short period every day with heavy guns. Owing, however, to their passion for order and method, the bombardment always commenced and ceased at approximately the same hours, so that it was customary to vacate all billets a short time prior to the zero hour and move out into the open country and wait there until such time as the "strafe" should cease, and then return and reckon upon being left unmolested for another period of twenty-four hours. This arrangement worked excellently for a few days, but then the enemy did a most unsporting thing—he changed his bombardment time! Suddenly, without warning, a heavy shell crashed through the walls of a large barn in which the men of "A" Squadron were billeted, resulting in three men being wounded and a mule killed. Another shell exploded close to the house in which the Commanding Officer and Adjutant were billeted, and as the former was at the moment engaged in his ablutions, his hurried exit, clad in a bath towel, afforded a comic element to the incident. The regiment remained at Rouge Croix until the 16th and then received orders to rejoin the Brigade at Vieille Chapelle. On arrival it was met by the Brigadier, who expressed great pleasure at the smart and fit appearance of the men. The horses were now received back from the Jodhpur Lancers, in whose charge they had been left, and on the 17th November the whole Brigade moved into a fresh billeting area in the vicinity of Essars and Béthune, the latter being a dismal town of mean streets and depressing houses. The Germans shelled it daily from the neighbourhood of La Bassée, some seven miles away, but although a certain amount of material damage was done there were not many casualties.

On the night of 18th/19th snow fell heavily—a new experience for the majority of the men and also for the horses, although it was remarkable how quickly the latter adapted themselves to the rapid change of climate, considering that only some six weeks previously they had been sweltering in the heat of the Red Sea and now they were standing out in the open, covered with snow. As the Brigade was not, pending the arrival of reinforcements, required to act mounted, the horses' coats were allowed to grow, and grow they did! So much so that many of them soon resembled long-haired goats!

"Cold, biting winds and continuous rain" describes the climatic conditions during the first half of November, after which snow set in, and by the 20th the whole country lay under a white mantle. Although still wearing Indian khaki drill, the issue of woollen jerseys and gifts of mufflers, thick socks, and warm gloves from friends and well-wishers in England enabled the men to withstand the cold without suffering ill-health; in fact, the daily average of sick was less during these winter months than the normal in India.

On the 19th the regiment was visited by H.R.H. Prince

Arthur of Connaught, accompanied by the Corps Commander (General Sir James Willcocks), and on the 21st a composite squadron received the honour of being inspected by H.R.H. The Prince of Wales.

Owing to the heavy casualties suffered by the Lahore and Meerut Divisions in the front line and to the lack of reinforcements, it was found necessary to make use of the cavalry in the trenches in order to give their comrades in the infantry a little rest. Consequently on the 24th November the Secunderabad Cavalry Brigade was ordered to take over a portion of the line in the vicinity of Festubert, and a strong detachment from " B " and " D " Squadrons (under Major Adams) was detailed as the regimental quota for this duty. On their way up to the front line large numbers of wounded infantry were met, from whom it was ascertained that a counter-attack had just been carried out, as a result of which the Germans had been driven out of a portion of our trench line which had been captured by them earlier in the day.

The regimental detachment was now ordered to occupy that portion of the trench which had been recaptured (with the Poona Horse on its left).

" B " and " D " Squadrons were relieved a few days later by a similar detachment from " A " and " C " Squadrons (under Major Tennant), who held the line up to the night of 3rd/4th December, when the whole Brigade was withdrawn from the firing line and moved to a new billeting area a few miles east of Lillers, where, for the first time since landing in France, it was found possible to secure overhead shelter for the horses.

During this period of duty in the trenches the following casualties were incurred: Jemadar Fiazuddin seriously wounded, one sowar killed, eleven sowars wounded.

On the 5th December the following Special Order of the

Day by His Majesty King George V was published :—

"Officers, Non-commissioned Officers and Men.

"I am very glad to have been able to see my Army in the field. I much wished to do so, in order to gain a slight experience of the life you are leading. I wish I could have spoken to you all, to express my admiration of the splendid manner in which you have fought, and are still fighting, against a powerful and relentless enemy. By your discipline, pluck and endurance, inspired by the indomitable regimental spirit, you have not only upheld the tradition of the British Army, but added fresh lustre to its history.

"I was particularly struck by your soldierly, healthy, cheerful appearance.

"I cannot share your trials, dangers and successes, but I can assure you of the proud confidence and gratitude of myself and your fellow-countrymen.

"We follow you in our daily thoughts on your certain road to victory.

"GEORGE R.I."

A few days later all ranks were thrilled by the receipt of personal greetings and remembrances from Their Majesties the King and Queen and also from H.R.H. Princess Mary (now the Princess Royal). These consisted of : Christmas cards from Their Majesties King George V and Queen Mary; a Christmas card from H.R.H. Princess Mary together with a gilt metal box, embossed with a portrait of Her Royal Highness on the cover and containing a pipe, tobacco and cigarettes.

A brief description may now be given regarding the nature of the country, the defence of which had been entrusted to the Indian Army Corps.

Picture a dismal water-logged plain, intersected with patches of marshland and dotted about with a few isolated farmhouses and clumps of trees, the whole overhung with heavy mists which were seldom dispelled for more than a few hours in the afternoon. This dull, monotonous land boasted no hills and valleys, not even a mound. It was just a flat, dreary expanse. Even the main roads were only metalled in the centre, and the fields, being intersected with deep ditches full of water, made inter-communication very difficult.

Owing to the water-logged condition of the country, all reliefs had to be effected after dark, across the open, and the same applied to ration parties and stretcher-bearers carrying back the wounded. Even the very soil was unfriendly, resembling in consistency a mixture of grey mud and glue, clinging to everything touched, and it was only by exercising the greatest care that the rifle barrels and bolt actions were kept clean and in serviceable order. Another difficulty with which to contend was the bayonets. These did not fit and shook off after rapid fire, due to the fact that an old-pattern bayonet had been issued with the latest-pattern rifle. The G.O.C. Sirhind Brigade brought this to notice in a special report stating: " These points are borne out by all officers who have served in the fire trenches. The result was that when the Germans reached the fire trenches many men had no weapons to fight them with."

The trenches themselves (at any rate in the sector allotted to the regiment) were for the most part in a deplorable condition. Originally, no doubt, they had been suitably constructed, but the snow and frost, followed by a thaw and torrents of rain, caused the walls to disintegrate and the bottom was converted into a mud channel into which the men's feet sank, so that they could no longer fire over the top. In order to remedy this, earth (or rather sticky, glutinous clay) was dug out of the rear wall of the trench to provide a firing platform. This revealed a new horror, for it was found that the foundations of the rear wall contained the dead bodies of fallen soldiers in an advanced stage of decomposition, the stench from which was appalling. These corpses had to be removed when found and reburied after dark in the open ground behind. This removal of soil from the rear of the trench caused the walls to disintegrate still further and to fill the bed of the trench with more mud, which in its turn had to be removed; and so the process continued until the trenches became over six feet wide and thus afforded a nice, easy target for the German hand grenades and trench mortars. To remedy this deplorable state of affairs only two courses were open : either to revet the walls and raise the floor of the trenches (with sandbags, planks, brushwood, etc.), or to abandon them and construct new ones. Unfortunately, at this time, neither sandbags nor any other revetting materials were obtainable and, as a new trench line could not be constructed in the absence of orders and without a co-ordinated plan, the only thing to do was to continue digging out footholes in the front wall to enable the men to fire over the top, thereby widening the trench still further and making it a bigger shell-trap.

It was probably due to the numerical weakness of the Corps, and the consequent necessity for reducing the casualty list, that no attempts to capture portions of the enemy trenches were permitted during this period, but it was most unfortunate as the enemy were seen to be constructing saps up to our line with the intention of blowing it up with mines, which they succeeded in doing a few weeks later.

The Germans, although exposed to the same weather conditions, were very much better provided for in the matter of trench construction. They had ample supplies of revetting material and their parapet was heavily sandbagged and, in addition, they had steel plates built into the parapet, with loopholes cut in the centre, through which to fire. They also had large supplies of hand grenades and trench mortars, of which we had none. It is true that the British Sappers did their best to remedy the deficiency in hand grenades by utilizing empty jam tins and filling them with explosive and old bits of iron, broken glass, nails, etc., but these had to be exploded by time fuses, and it required very careful calculation in order to ascertain the right moment at which to throw them over. If too much time were allowed the Germans were enabled to pick them up and throw them back to explode in the trench from whence they originated; if too little time were allowed they burst in the thrower's hand.

A still greater handicap was the lamentable shortage of machine guns and artillery ammunition. As regards the latter, a particular incident may be described by way of illustration. The position of a German machine gun, which was causing much annoyance, had been located and a request was made to have this dislodged by artillery fire. An officer was sent from the trenches to the artillery observation post to point out the exact position of this machine gun, and the Battery Commander arranged that he would open fire at a specified time, the officer in the trench spotting for him. At the agreed moment the battery fired one round—this was signalled back "twenty yards over." The next round was again over, the third round was a yard or two short, and the fourth round, correct in distance, was a few yards to the right. Everyone was now expecting that the fifth round would destroy the pestiferous machine gun, but the Battery Commander phoned that he could not fire again as he had expended his daily allowance of ammunition!

On the 16th December Rissaldar Mahbub Khan I died suddenly of heart failure as he was mounting his horse. He was an excellent officer and much esteemed by all ranks. He was buried in Busnettes and a stone erected over his grave, the cost of which was subscribed for by the whole regiment. When Lieutenant-Colonel Tinley and Major Gregson visited the village in 1926 the stone was still there, but it is understood that it has since been removed to the Military Cemetery.

CHAPTER IV

19TH DECEMBER 1914 TO 31ST DECEMBER 1914

German Capture of Trenches at Festubert—Despatch of Secunderabad Cavalry Brigade as Reinforcements—Givenchy—Casualties—Gallantry of Captain Ross and Lieutenant Tinley—Formation of 2nd Indian Cavalry Division—Farewell Letter from General Willcocks.

THE Brigade having once more resumed its rôle as Corps Reserve (and, incidentally, the sole reserve available in the hands of the Corps Commander), it had to be maintained in a state of constant readiness and be prepared to move on the shortest notice.

At dawn on the 19th December the Germans launched a heavy attack against the whole weakly held front of the Indian Corps. The infantry—who had been in the trenches for some seven weeks on end—were tired out and the centre and left of the Lahore Division and the right centre of the Meerut Division were driven in. At these points saps had been dug by the Germans to within ten feet of the trench line and from these sap-heads mines, charged with fifty kilos of explosive, had been laid under the trenches. When these mines were exploded large gaps were created in the line and the position became most critical. In these circumstances the Corps Commander decided to bring up his reserve. At about 3 p.m. the Secunderabad Cavalry Brigade received orders to despatch as strong a force as possible to Annezin, a village some six miles away from the billeting area, " to be there by 6 p.m." Accordingly, a detachment composed of 7th Dragoon Guards (200 men), XXth Deccan Horse (200 men), 34th Poona Horse (165 men), Jodhpur Lancers (200 men), with the necessary complement of British and Indian Officers, was detailed, the whole being placed under the command of Lieutenant-Colonel Lemprière, 7th Dragoon Guards. It was close upon 4 p.m. before this order reached Squadron Commanders, just as preparations were being made for the evening meal. As the time for assembly at Annezin was fixed for 6 p.m. there was no time to spare and all uncooked rations had to be discarded. Any bread or biscuits on hand were hastily transferred to haversacks and, as things turned out, this was all the food the men had to live on for the next forty-eight hours.

Punctually at six o'clock the several detachments rode into the small town of Annezin and Colonel Lemprière went off to report his arrival. It was now quite dark and heavy rain was falling, but shelter was unobtainable. Orders were received to send back all horses to billets, and just before 8 p.m. the now dismounted detachment marched to the village of Essars, distant some three miles. Here it remained all night in the street, the men getting what shelter they could from the cold and wet by huddling together under the eaves of the houses. When day broke on the 20th the Brigade was still left without orders until close upon noon, when it was directed to march to the village of Gorre, about two miles distant, on the road to Festubert. Every now and then a stray shell burst in the village and ambulance wagons came rushing through from the front, bringing back the wounded, but no information was obtainable as to what the situation was or why the Brigade was collected at Gorre. Not until close upon 4 p.m., just as it was getting dark, did a staff officer arrive with orders for the detachment to advance and occupy the second-line trenches, which lay about a mile to the front. After tramping over wet, muddy fields, in the now pitch darkness, these were eventually found, but as there was about a foot of liquid mud in them and the cold was intense, conditions were none too cheerful. No information was given as to the extent of frontage each regiment was to hold or which units, if any, lay on their flanks.

At about 10 p.m. an order was passed down the trench that the detachments were to re-form as quickly as possible on the main road and, as soon as the various units were assembled, an advance was made to the vicinity of the village of Le Plantin, which was some two miles distant and just behind the front line. On arrival, orders were received to occupy the breastworks forming the intermediate line. This being situated in the marshland around Le Plantin, trenches could not be dug and so no cover from shell fire was obtainable.

Hardly had the line of breastworks been occupied than fresh orders were received to evacuate them and re-form on the road in the rear of the village of Festubert. As the 8th Gurkhas were also assembled here, there was some congestion on the road and, owing to the pitch darkness, a certain amount of confusion of units. At about 3.30 a.m. on the 21st Major Tennant, commanding the regimental detachment, was directed to return to Le Plantin and report to the G.O.C. Bareilly Brigade for orders. Whilst proceeding there he was met by Brigadier-General Wadeson and told to return to his unit as fast as possible as an attack upon the German trench line had been ordered to commence almost immediately.

The order for the attack was as follows :—

"Orders issued by Major-General Macbean, C.B., C.V.O., at 3.45 a.m. on 21st December.

"1. The enemy has seized and is occupying the trenches originally occupied by Sirhind Brigade.

"2. The G.O.C. will deliver a counter-attack to recover these trenches and hold them.

"3. The attack will be delivered at 4.30 a.m. as follows :—
   (a) 2/8 Gurkhas will advance on the abandoned trenches on a front of 300 paces, with their right resting on the left communication trench of right section.

(*b*) Secunderabad Cavalry Brigade will prolong to the left of 2/8 Gurkhas and advance on a front of 450 paces, taking their direction from 2/8 Gurkhas.

"As soon as the trenches are reached, the 2/8 Gurkhas will clear the trenches to their right of the enemy and the Secunderabad Cavalry Brigade to their left."

In addition, Brigadier-General Wadeson issued the following verbal orders :—

"The attack to be carried out in two lines at 200 yards distance.

"The Poona Horse—on the left—to be disposed in two lines. The XXth Deccan Horse—all in the front line—on the right of the Poona Horse and to maintain touch on their right with the 2/8 Gurkhas, who will direct the advance.

"The Jodhpur Lancers, in the 2nd line—in support of the XXth Deccan Horse.

"The attack to be made with the bayonet and no firing or cheering to be allowed."

By the time these orders had been issued to Squadron Commanders and explained to Indian Officers it was past 4.30 a.m., at which hour the attack had been ordered to commence, so that there was no time available for making a preliminary reconnaissance of the ground to be crossed. Nor was it possible, owing to the darkness, to indicate the location or extent of the position held by the enemy or upon which point to concentrate the attack. The regiment marched through the village of Le Plantin and as soon as the open country beyond was reached Major Tennant ordered " A " Squadron, which was leading, to deploy to the right and gain touch with the 2nd/8th Gurkhas; " C " Squadron, which followed, to deploy to the left of " A "; and " D " Squadron, which came last, to deploy on the left of " C " and obtain touch with the Poona Horse. This successive deployment resulted in the advance of the regiment being made in echelon instead of in line, as "A" Squadron had to conform to the movements of the 2nd/8th Gurkhas and thus could not wait for the other squadrons to come up.

Owing to the intense darkness it was impossible to obtain a general view of the progress of this attack, but the light shed by the enemy's Very pistols and star shells enabled one to get momentary glimpses of small groups of officers and men crawling along, crossing deep, wide ditches and cutting passages through the barbed wire, and all the time being subjected to severe fire from artillery, machine guns and rifles. Cohesion was impossible on account of the nature of the ground and the darkness. Units got mixed up in the endeavour to gain touch with the bodies on their flanks and but for the light from the flashes of the enemy rifles, direction would inevitably have been lost. In spite of everything the advance continued, but the nearer the attacking troops approached the German position the more intense became the firing, more particularly from the flanks, and men could be seen falling all round. A few groups of men actually reached the German trenches, but with no supports behind them they were speedily overwhelmed, and as the break of dawn now disclosed the fact that no fresh troops were advancing in support either on the flanks or from the rear, and as five out of the six British and five out of the seven Indian Officers had been either killed or wounded, it was rightly judged that to prolong the attack further could only result in useless slaughter and so the order was given to retire. Owing to the fast approach of daylight the retirement had to be carried out under the greatest difficulty in order to avoid heavy losses. That this was successfully effected is evidence of the courage and discipline shown by all concerned. When it is recalled that for the past thirty-six hours the men had had no sleep and, beyond some sodden biscuits carried in the haversacks, nothing to eat, and that during that period they had been kept standing about soaked to the skin and frozen with cold, and furthermore that their sole weapon was the bayonet, in the use of which they were unskilled, and which fitted the rifles so insecurely that many of the men resorted to binding them on with bits of string and old rags, it is a matter of legitimate pride to realize how splendidly they acquitted themselves on this, their very first experience of actual warfare. The attack was carried out in strict accordance with the orders received with no firing and no cheering and from first to last there was never one moment's hesitation.

The gallantry displayed by all ranks on this occasion was held to be so outstanding that the name "Givenchy" was subsequently awarded to the regiment as a Battle Honour.

The Corps Commander, General Sir James Willcocks, in commenting upon this attack, says :—*

"*It was a hopeless attempt;* the ground was deep in mud and a network of ditches and the enemy's fire very heavy. Nevertheless these gallant troops actually reached and entered our abandoned trenches, but were then subjected to a heavy flanking fire, and occasionally to that of our own guns. Under such conditions it was no wonder they were driven back to their starting point and suffered severely."

In his official report, Brigadier-General Wadeson made the following remarks :—

"The attack, once launched, made fair progress, until heavy machine-gun fire from the flanks obliged the detachments to fall back. Small parties succeeded in reaching the hostile trenches, but the lack of sufficient depth prevented the attack being pushed home.

* * * * * *

"I wish to place on record that the officers and men under my command behaved in a most exemplary manner throughout these trying operations and that the failure of the attack at

---
* *With the Indians in France*, p. 171.

Festubert was entirely due to circumstances over which they had no control."

Although the original strength of the regimental detachment which assembled at Annezin amounted to 200 rank and file, owing to the horses having to be sent back to billets the actual numbers participating in this attack only totalled 6 British Officers, 7 Indian Officers, 160 rank and file, and the casualties, amounting to forty-four per cent., were as follows :—

British Officers.—Captains J. S. McEuen and C. A. C. Mackenzie, killed; Major E. Tennant and Captain C. Jarvis, severely wounded; Lieutenant F. B. N. Tinley, slightly wounded.

Indian Officers.—Rissaldar-Major Jhermal Singh, Rissaldar Mir Hadayat Ali and Ressaidar Mahbub Khan II, killed; Rissaldar Amir Mohammed Khan and Jemadar Mangal Singh, severely wounded (the former subsequently died of his wounds, but survived long enough to be promoted Rissaldar-Major).

		"A" Squadron.	"C" Squadron.	"D" Squadron.
British Officers—	Killed	0	2	0
	Wounded	2	1	0
Indian Officers—	Killed	1	2	0
	Wounded	1	0	1
Non-commissioned Officers—				
	Killed	7	2	5
	Wounded	5	3	1
Sowars—	Killed	11	9	6
	Wounded	12	4	6
	Total	39	23	19

Note.—" B " Squadron was left at Regimental Headquarters in charge of the horses.

The disparity in the Squadron casualty lists is probably due to the fact that " A " Squadron, being the first to deploy and obliged to move forward in conformity with the Gurkhas on its right, received the concentrated fire of the enemy before the other squadrons got up into line.

The loss of Captains McEuen and Mackenzie, both excellent and much-esteemed officers, was a sad blow, and with Major Tennant and Captain Jarvis evacuated to England—severely wounded—the number of British Officers left with the regiment was reduced to one per squadron. In addition to this, five Indian Officers out of seven, and twenty-three non-commissioned officers were included in the casualty list so that, for the time being, the efficiency of the regiment was severely impaired. The deaths of Rissaldar-Major Jhermal Singh, Rissaldar Hadayat Ali, and Ressaidar Mahbub Khan II were greatly deplored; Mir Hadayat Ali was in his thirty-third year of service, a most gallant old soldier to the end.

The remnant of the regiment was rallied in the village of Festubert by Captain Ross (the only British Officer who had escaped scatheless) and during the process he performed a gallant deed for which he was subsequently awarded the Distinguished Service Order. Rissaldar Amir Mohammed Khan of his squadron was severely wounded in the thigh and, being quite unable to move, called out for assistance. Duffadars Sardar Singh and Shanka Rao at once ran to him and dragged him back a short distance. They were then joined by Captain Ross and together they managed to pull him into a ditch, where he was protected from the enemy rifle fire. Leaving the two non-commissioned officers with the wounded Indian Officer, Captain Ross ran back to get a stretcher, but being unable to find one he rejoined the party and, although it was now daylight, the three of them succeeded in carrying Amir Mohammed Khan to safety.

A similar act of bravery was performed by Lieutenant Tinley and Kote-Duffadar Abdul Gafoor Khan of the Poona Horse. Captain Grimshaw of the Poona Horse had been seen to fall, badly wounded, by the Kote-Duffadar, who promptly ran to his aid and dragged him into a hollow close by. When the order came to retire, Captain Grimshaw had become embedded in the mud and the Kote-Duffadar could not move him. Lieutenant Tinley then ran up to them and, although it was now broad daylight and the spot close up to the German trench, from which they must have presented a conspicuous target, Captain Grimshaw was picked up and carried back to a position of safety behind the line. For this gallant conduct Lieutenant Tinley was subsequently awarded the Military Cross.

In view of the possibility of the Germans making a fresh attack, the remnant of the Brigade, under the command of Brigadier-General Wadeson, was re-formed and marched back to the intermediate line of trenches (a short distance behind the line Le Plantin–Festubert), and occupied these until the morning of the 22nd December. It then moved to the village of Festubert and remained there, in a state of readiness, until the evening when, the troops of the Corps under General Sir Douglas Haig having arrived and taken over the whole front of the Indian Army Corps, the detachment was ordered to return to billets. As these were some eighteen miles distant and both officers and men were utterly worn out from want of food and sleep, the Brigadier wisely varied the order by marching back only a short distance and getting the troops under shelter for the night along the Rue de Béthune. On the morning of the 23rd December the march was continued as far as Gorre, where some motor lorries were commandeered and the detachment was conveyed in these to the new billeting area in the vicinity of Mazinghem.

The 9th Secunderabad Cavalry Brigade now ceased to form the Mobile Reserve of the Indian Army Corps and became incorporated in the 2nd Indian Cavalry Division, under the command of Major-General G. A. Cookson, C.B., which also included the Mhow and Meerut Cavalry Brigades. The 1st Cavalry Division comprised the Ambala-Lucknow and Sialkote Cavalry Brigades, and the two Divisions formed the Indian

GIVENCHY

- A. Front Line Trench.
- B. Intermediate Line.
- C. Second Line or Reserve Trench.
- D. German Line.

KILOMETRES.

Royal Deccan Horse

Facing page 32

Cavalry Corps, under the command of Lieutenant-General M. F. Rimington—a former Inspector-General of Cavalry in India.

In bidding farewell to the Brigade, the Corps Commander, General Sir James Willcocks, issued the following order:—

"As the Secunderabad Cavalry Brigade has now left this Corps, I write to convey my best thanks to Brigadier-General Wadeson for the great assistance he has always given us. His troops have not only always been ready to turn out at a moment's notice, but have taken a full share in the trenches and in digging the 2nd Defensive Line. The discipline, endurance and cheerfulness of his regular regiments and the Jodhpur Lancers have been a fine example and I owe a debt of gratitude to all ranks for their cordial assistance whenever called for. I shall not fail to bring this to the notice of the Field-Marshal Commander-in-Chief."

CHAPTER V

1915

Inspections—Neuve Chapelle—Belgian Frontier—Visit of Their Majesties the King and Queen of the Belgians—Loos—Departure of Indian Infantry for Mesopotamia.

WITH the opening of the New Year reinforcements commenced to arrive from the Base Depot at Marseilles to make good the losses sustained at Festubert and previously. As regards British Officers, some came from those regiments of Indian cavalry not yet detailed for active service, others from the Indian Army Reserve, and in addition, as an experiment, some junior officers of the British Yeomanry were attached for duty. These latter quickly picked up sufficient Hindustani to make themselves understood and did their utmost to identify themselves with the regiment.

As regards the drafts of rank and file from India, a large proportion consisted of recently enlisted recruits, so that every spare moment had to be devoted to troop and squadron training and musketry in order to fit them to take their place in the ranks. Unfortunately, the spare moments for this essential work were few and far between, as throughout the month of January the Brigade was given a surfeit of training in night attacks (as the result of Givenchy), interspersed with route marching, entrenching, bayonet fighting, and numerous inspections by Army, Corps and Divisional Commanders.

On the 11th January the 2nd Indian Cavalry Division was inspected by the Divisional Commander, Major-General Cookson.

On the 18th January the whole of the Indian Cavalry Corps —consisting of nineteen regiments (six British and thirteen

Indian) and six batteries Royal Horse Artillery—under the command of Lieutenant-General Rimington, was concentrated on some rising ground near Enguinegette (reputed to be the site of the Battle of Spurs in 1513), for inspection by the Army Corps Commander, General Sir James Willcocks.

On the 28th January the regiment, in company with the other units of the Division, was again paraded for inspection by the Cavalry Corps Commander, General Rimington.

Training was continued through the month of February and on the 11th a Brigade tactical exercise (rear-guard action) was attended by H.R.H. The Prince of Wales, the Corps and Divisional Commanders also being present. On the 27th the whole Cavalry Division executed a route march, covering about thirty miles.

With the commencement of spring, hopes ran high that an opportunity would soon be given to the cavalry to engage the enemy. The infantry of the Indian Corps were holding the line from Givenchy to Neuve Chapelle and orders had been issued for an attack to be made by the whole of the Indian and IV Corps upon the village of Neuve Chapelle and the Bois de Biez—still in the hands of the Germans. In order to reap the full benefit of success the cavalry—*i.e.*, both the British and Indian Cavalry Corps—were instructed to be ready to advance through the gap in the enemy's front opposite Neuve Chapelle, as soon as a passage across the German trenches could be prepared. This subsequent action was to take the form of a wheel along the ridge into the open country, behind the German lines, between Neuve Chapelle and La Bassée.

On the 10th March the two attacking Corps carried Neuve Chapelle, and during the night of 10th/11th March the Secunderabad Cavalry Brigade moved up to Allouagne and thence into the wood of Le Marguet, where it remained concealed and in a state of readiness throughout the 11th.

However, the battle ended on the following day and as no sufficient gap had been made in the enemy's defence line to enable the cavalry to break through, the latter were ordered to return to their billeting areas.

On the 7th March Duffadars Sardar Singh and Shunker Rao were awarded the Indian Order of Merit, Second Class, and Sowar Gokal Singh the Indian Distinguished Service Medal, for "conspicuous gallantry in rescuing, under a most destructive fire, Rissaldar Amir Mohammed Khan at Festubert on the 21st December, 1914."

On the 14th March the regiment left Mazinghem, where it had been billeted since the previous December, and moved to fresh billets near Enguinegette. These, however, being insanitary, were vacated on the 17th and the regiment moved to new billets at Crecques. About this time (March) it was notified that the Government of India had sanctioned a twenty-five per cent. increase of pay to all Indian ranks, to have effect from the date of landing in France.

On the 24th March yet another divisional inspection parade was held—this time for the benefit of certain foreign officers of exalted rank.

During March digging parties, two hundred strong, were furnished by the regiment to assist in preparing a defensive line at Robecq. These detachments were taken to and fro by motor lorries and employed for eight hours each day in digging trenches.

From the 12th to the 14th April a detachment of four British Officers and 200 rank and file was employed in trench making in the vicinity of St. Venant.

On the 21st April the Division was paraded once more for inspection—this time for the United States Military Attachés.

On the 22nd April the Germans opened their attack on Hill 60, in the neighbourhood of Ypres. To counter this the 2nd

Indian Cavalry Division was hurriedly moved up to the Belgian frontier.

On the 24th the regiment marched to the Brigade rendezvous at Mametz, and thence the Cavalry Division complete advanced to the neighbourhood of Cassel and Watou, the regiment reaching its billets at Zuytpeene at 10 p.m. that night. The whole of the next day horses were kept saddled up and ready to move at any moment, but in the evening permission was given to off-saddle and return to billets, with the proviso to be ready to move at an hour's notice. No further advance was made, however, until the 28th, when the regiment marched via Wemaers, Oudezeele and Hout Kerque (over the Belgian frontier) to billets near Proven, the weather being fine and sunny.

On the 1st May reconnaissances of the Poperinghe Canal were carried out, from Woesten to Eykhoek, and at dawn the regiment returned to Zuytpeene.

On the night of 4th/5th May the regiment marched via Blaringhem and Aire to Laires, a distance of about thirty miles, arriving at the latter place about 9 a.m. on the 5th, and went into billets, with orders to be ready to move at three hours' notice.

On the 17th May a move was made to Lapugnoy, some ten miles from La Bassée, and on the 20th the regiment returned to its former billets at Laires. Whilst at Laires the following autograph letter was received by the regiment from the Corps Commander, General Sir James Willcocks, in reply to one congratulating him upon his recent decoration as Grand Officer of the Legion of Honour :—

"I heartily thank the officers and men of the XXth Deccan Horse for their kind congratulations. I will always remember their fine soldierly conduct during the trying days of November and December 1914 and the great help they always gave the Army Corps."

It will be of interest to mention that during this month the following order was circulated by the Cavalry Corps Commander to all cavalry regiments :—

"Patrols should invariably carry their swords, not their rifles, in their hands, ready for immediate use. On meeting a hostile patrol, even of superior numbers, they should charge at once, at the gallop. These tactics have proved universally successful."

Another order of interest which was issued during this month was to the effect that in future the Rissaldar-Major was to be relieved of all troop duties and be attached to the Commanding Officer's staff as his confidential adviser on all matters affecting the discipline and interior administration of the regiment.

On the 13th June a divisional ceremonial parade was held at Linghem for Their Majesties the King and Queen of the Belgians. This was followed by a display of tent-pegging and trick riding. Their Majesties expressed much pleasure at what they had seen and sent a generous present of 10,000 cigarettes and some sugar to the regiment as a mark of their appreciation.

It was during this month that the new-pattern thrusting sword (the present of H.E.H. The Nizam of Hyderabad) was received from Messrs. Wilkinson & Co. These swords were inspected by the Cavalry Corps Commander and met with his entire approval.

On the 26th June the regiment moved from Laires, where it had been quartered for nearly two months, to new billets at Mazinghem, and whilst here Lieutenant F. B. N. Tinley was awarded the Military Cross "for conspicuous gallantry in leading his men in the attack on the German trenches at Festubert on the morning of 21st December 1914 and gallantly assisting Captain Grimshaw and a sowar of the Poona Horse, both being wounded, to a place of safety, under heavy fire, himself being already wounded in the face."

During the whole of July the regiment furnished strong detachments for digging a second line of trenches in the vicinity of Vermelles. These detachments were absent for several days at a time and were billeted at Les Brébis during their tour of duty. The Officer Commanding Royal Engineers was good enough to express "his particular satisfaction with the excellent work done by the XXth Deccan Horse, it being much above the average."

On the 18th a composite squadron, under Captain R. B. Worgan, attended a divisional parade for inspection by Field-Marshal Lord Kitchener at Mazinghem.

About this time an order was received directing that all British Officers' personal servants were to return to India, their places being taken by soldier servants detailed from British regiments. This was a great deprivation and it is difficult to see what benefit was gained.

On the 1st August the regiment was moved from Mazinghem to St. Pierre à Gouy, ten miles from Amiens, and, in order to allow their comrades in the infantry a period of rest prior to the projected Battle of Loos, the whole of the Indian Cavalry Corps were given a tour of duty in the front-line trenches. The portion allotted to the regiment was the section facing Thiepval, and on the 8th August they took over the trenches held by the Seaforth Highlanders and the Argyll and Sutherland Highlanders. This portion of the line was close to the German trenches and was subjected to constant attention from *minenwerfers*, which destroyed portions of the trenches and wire entanglements but caused few casualties—only fourteen men in all being wounded.

On the 20th August General Cookson, commanding the 2nd Indian Cavalry Division, sent the following letter to Major Adams, who was temporarily in command of the regiment (Colonel Elsmie acting as Brigade Commander):—

"Just a few lines to let you know how pleased I was with the work done by the regiment under your command, particularly the work under Captain Worgan, of repairing 15 feet of parapet last night. I greatly liked that connecting trench to 18th on your right and the 2nd line made in case of the salient being mined.

"Will you please convey my great appreciation to Officers, Indian Officers, N.C.Os. and men.

"It was very nice to find everyone so cheery and ready to work."

The following officers were subsequently mentioned in Despatches for coolness under fire and general good example: Captain R. B. Worgan and Jemadar Sher Singh.

The Brigade was relieved on the night of 22nd/23rd August and marched to Frechencourt, about eight miles in rear of the trench line. From now on to the end of the month the regiment was engaged in digging a reserve line of trenches in the neighbourhood of Senlis.

On the 29th August the Colonel received the following communication from Brigade Headquarters:—

"The G.O.C. directs me to inform you that he much appreciates the praiseworthy manner in which the British Officers, Indian Officers, and men of the Deccan Horse carried out their duties in the trenches from the 12th to the 23rd August."

On the 31st August a reinforcement of one hundred rank and file under Second-Lieutenants Rayneau and Rust (both Indian Army Reserve) joined the regiment from Marseilles, the strength of all Indian cavalry units being temporarily increased to 16 British Officers, 18 Indian Officers, 575 rank and file.

During this month gas masks were issued to the regiment and lessons given in their use, adjustment, etc., and also in passing through gas whilst wearing them.

On the 1st September the Secunderabad Cavalry Brigade relieved the Lucknow Cavalry Brigade in the trenches near Authuille and held these until the 13th when, upon relief, the regiment marched to billets at Hangest, on the Somme between Abbeville and Amiens.

On the 21st the Division was inspected by Field-Marshal Lord Kitchener near St. Ouen and he remarked upon the smart appearance of the regiment.

On the 22nd the cavalry again moved forward to a line north of Amiens, the regiment being billeted at Fienvillers.

During this month each cavalry regiment was provided with two Vickers machine guns in addition to the two Maxims already in its possession.

The whole of the Indian Cavalry Corps was now concentrated in the vicinity of Doullens, ready to co-operate with the British and French cavalry in exploiting any success that might be gained at the Battle of Loos, which was now in progress, but unfortunately no opportunity occurred for utilizing their services.

On the 14th October the Division was inspected by the General Officer Commanding the French Cavalry Corps, with whom we should have co-operated had a break-through at Loos been feasible.

On the 22nd October the Brigade moved into winter quarters in the neighbourhood of Abbeville—the regiment being billeted at Pont Remy—and whilst here was issued with a supply of Mills hand grenades.

On the 9th November the following intimation was published :—

" The Corps Commander has pleasure in announcing that the Field Marshal Commander-in-Chief has approved of the distribution of French decorations to officers and other ranks of the 2nd Indian Cavalry Division, as undermentioned, for good service and devotion to duty in the field :—

XXth Deccan Horse:

Lt.-Colonel G. E. D. Elsmie, 4th Class Legion of Honour.
Duffadar Bhawani Singh ... Médaille Militaire.
Kote Duffadar Sirdar Singh } Croix de Guerre."
Duffadar Shankar Rao ...

On the 11th November the Indian Cavalry Corps was paraded for inspection by the Third Army Commander, Lieutenant-General Allenby, who distributed the above-mentioned decorations and subsequently issued the following order :—

" The Army Commander wishes that all ranks may know how highly he appreciates the efficiency of this splendid body of Cavalry and he hopes that the time may soon come when the conditions of warfare may enable the Indian Cavalry Corps to show their prowess in the open field."

On 18th November the regiment moved from Pont Remy to Liercourt.

Nothing of interest occurred during the month of December beyond the fact that on the 17th the regiment was moved to new billets at Limercourt and Huppy.

The year 1915 was, from a cavalry point of view, uneventful and in consequence somewhat depressing for all cavalry soldiers. The trench warfare on the Western Front entirely precluded all possibility of mounted enterprise. On four occasions the Cavalry Corps had been concentrated for possible action, viz. : during the Battles of Neuve Chapelle, Hill 60, La Bassée, and Loos, but in no case had any opportunity arisen for cavalry to push through the German trenches. The only relief to the monotony of the year was when the Corps was twice used for trench work in the vicinity of Albert. Apart from this no fighting took place, but at the same time it is safe to say that on no previous occasion in its history had the regiment been more efficient or the horses and men more fit, as testified by the marked appreciation of the several inspecting General Officers.

Towards the later portion of the year the infantry units of the Indian Expeditionary Force were withdrawn from France and transferred to Mesopotamia. During the fifteen months that it had been actively engaged, the Indian Corps had sustained close upon 35,000 casualties, and the difficulties of obtaining reinforcements had become insuperable. It had gallantly performed its part and helped to hold the line during the time necessary to enable the new armies to be raised in England. With very few of their original officers left and the ranks filled with hastily trained recruits, it was time for the regiments to be withdrawn and given an opportunity to reorganize.

CHAPTER VI

1916

Cavalry Reorganization—St. Riquier—Somme Valley—Delville Wood—Formation of Cavalry Corps—Pioneer Companies.

ON the 6th January the Division paraded near Le Plouy for the Cavalry Corps Commander—Lieutenant-General M. Rimington—prior to his giving up the command. On the evening of the same day the Commanding Officer received the following telegram :—

"The G.O.C. wishes you to convey to the XXth Deccan Horse his appreciation of their appearance and work on parade this morning. Men and horses were looking well and in good hard condition. Turn-out was strong and movements carried out accurately and quietly."

On the 26th January Lieutenant-Colonel F. W. C. Turner, Second-in-Command, had the misfortune to be thrown from his horse (causing a fracture of his leg), which necessitated his being evacuated sick to England, and Major Adams took over his duties in the regiment.

On the 2nd February the regiment moved into new billets in the area Tours-en-Vimeu-Houden-Hanicourt. During this month the regimental machine-gun detachment was incorporated with the newly formed Brigade Machine Gun Squadron, and a regimental Grenadier Section of sixty-two men was formed and placed under the command of Captain Larkin.

During March many changes occurred : the Cavalry Corps ceased to form a separate command, each of the Cavalry Divisions being placed under the orders of Army Commanders, the 2nd Indian Cavalry Division being attached to the Fourth Army ;

General Cookson was succeeded in the command of the Division by Major-General Macandrew; and Brigadier-General Gregory succeeded Major-General Wadeson in the command of the Secunderabad Cavalry Brigade. In addition to the above, Lieutenant-Colonel Elsmie was transferred to the command of the 25th Cavalry in India and Major Adams took over the officiating command of the regiment.

About the middle of April the Brigade marched to St. Riquier, where a large tract of waste land had been made available by the French Government for cavalry tactical-training purposes, and spent ten days carrying out various tactical exercises, returning a fortnight later, on the 8th May, for a week's divisional training.

It was about this time that metal regimental badges were discarded and, in lieu, a patch of green and white material about two inches by one and a half inches was worn under the shoulder strap. Another innovation was the issue to the regiment of sixteen Hotchkiss guns—four per squadron, *i.e.*, one per troop.

On the 21st May, Lieutenant-Colonel E. Tennant rejoined the regiment from duty in England and took over the command.

On the 2nd June the regiment moved to Friaucourt and carried out troop and squadron drill on the sands in the vicinity of Tréport and Cayeux-sur-Mer, returning on the 8th to its former billets at Tours.

On the 16th the Canadian Cavalry Brigade joined the Division in place of the Meerut Cavalry Brigade, which was under orders to proceed to Egypt.

On the 22nd June the regiment marched to St. Riquier for Brigade and Divisional training, and on the 26th marched at 8 p.m. in pouring rain to Cissy, arriving at the latter place at 2 a.m. on the 27th. A halt was made here during the day and the march continued at 6 p.m. for Querrieu, which was reached about 1.30 a.m. on the 28th, the regiment bivouacking in the valley of the Hallue river.

On the 30th June the regiment was inspected by General Gough, the G.O.C. "Reserve" Army.

On the 1st July, the commencement of the Battle of the Somme, the Brigade marched at 3.30 a.m. in line of squadron columns to a position of readiness at Buire-sur-Ancre, arriving about 5.30 a.m., and remained there till the evening, when it returned to Pont Noyelles. The orders for the 2nd Indian Cavalry Division were to be ready to pass through the infantry, with Bapaume as its objective, should the attack be successful. The Secunderabad Cavalry Brigade was selected for the post of honour in leading the Division, with the 7th Dragoon Guards as advanced guard. One squadron of the Fort Garry Horse was attached to the Division with portable bridges to enable the trench line to be crossed, and four other Cavalry Divisions were ready to follow and make good any successes obtained; but, unfortunately, the infantry attack did not succeed in creating a gap in the German line and hence the services of the cavalry could not be utilized.

The regiment remained in bivouac at Pont Noyelles until the 13th July, when it marched to Dernancourt and bivouacked just south of Meaulte.

At 1.30 a.m. on the 14th the regiment marched in brigade to Bray-sur-Somme, arriving just before dawn. Here horses were watered and fed, and at 8.30 a.m. a further advance was made into the valley just south of Montauban. During this time the 2nd Infantry Division had succeeded in advancing, under cover of darkness, some thousand yards in front of their own front-line trenches, and at 3.25 a.m. they commenced an attack on the front extending from Longueval on the right to Bazentin-le-Petit on the left.

Heavy fighting continued throughout the day, and towards

the evening the German resistance appeared to be weakening. The opportunity could only be a fleeting one and therefore it was decided to take the risk of sending forward the whole of the Cavalry Division in an attempt to break through and trust to the infantry supports being able to arrive in time to make good any positions that might be captured. However, it was learnt, just about the moment when the Secunderabad Cavalry Brigade left Sabot Copse, that the supports could not arrive for several hours, and therefore the orders for the advance of the remainder of the Cavalry Division were cancelled.

The Secunderabad Cavalry Brigade, having been selected to act as advanced guard, received orders at 5.30 p.m. to advance and co-operate with the 9th and 22nd Infantry Divisions, who were about to attack the enemy holding High Wood and Delville Wood. The Brigade moved to a position of assembly near Sabot Copse, and there the regiment received the following orders :—

"Move at once, with your right on line cross-roads 250 yards North of *V* in Longueval and S.11 Central, into a position to attack Delville Wood from the N. and N.W., so as to enable the 9th Division to complete the capture of that place.

"Your left via the Quarry in S.22 C and Windmill 300 yards N. of *G* in Longueval. On arriving on the ridge in S.11 push forward strong patrols towards Flers. Be sure to maintain communication with the 7th Dragoon Guards on your left and also with the 9th Division on your right. G.O.C. will move slightly to the rear of and between you and 7th Dragoon Guards."

In compliance with these orders "A" Squadron, under Captain Jarvis, was detailed as advanced guard to the regiment with its objective the high ground in Square 11 (see Map facing p. 52). Unfortunately, the only passage through our lines from the assembly position at Sabot Copse was over a rough and narrow track which necessitated the advance being made in half-sections for a considerable distance and, as the 7th Dragoon Guards were leading, there was some delay before the regiment could get through. As it passed through the defile cheers were raised by the gunners and infantry, as this was the first chance that the cavalry had had of acting mounted since the commencement of trench warfare.

As each squadron cleared the defile it formed line and advanced at a gallop in the direction taken by the advanced guard, which lay through a broad belt of standing corn, in which small parties of the enemy lay concealed. Individual Germans now commenced popping up on all sides, throwing up their arms and shouting " Kamerad," and not a few, evidently under the impression that no quarter would be given, flung their arms around the horses' necks and begged for mercy— all of which impeded the advance. It was about this time that one of our aeroplanes came over, flying very low and firing tracer bullets to show the positions of hostile machine guns and also that of a German trench which ran from High Wood to Delville Wood and which, owing to the corn, was quite invisible.

When the advanced guard reached its objective, a German trench to the north of Delville Wood, occupied by infantry, could be seen clearly and German artillery (located by the flash of the guns) opened fire from a point near Square 6.

During the whole period of the advance the regiment had been exposed to flanking machine-gun fire from Delville Wood; consequently " C " Squadron was ordered to form a defensive flank upon the right of " A " Squadron, and " D " Squadron was moved up to occupy the gap between the regiment and the 7th Dragoon Guards, who appeared to be held up some distance south of High Wood. " B " Squadron was retained in a central position as a support in case of unforeseen eventualities.

The Brigadier had specified that communication was to be maintained with the 7th Dragoon Guards on the left and the 9th Division on the right. As no touch could be obtained with the 9th Division, whose whereabouts were unknown, and as any further advance of the regiment to a position from which to attack Delville Wood from the north would separate it still further from the 7th Dragoon Guards, messages were sent back to the Brigadier asking for instructions, but unfortunately he could not be found.

Captain Jarvis now reported that bodies of Germans were massing on his right front, as though preparing for a counter-attack, and consequently "B" Squadron was warned to be ready to act at any moment. The German attack, however, did not materialize. It had now become dark and as the left flank of the regiment was in the air, whilst the right flank, "C" Squadron, was under heavy fire from Delville Wood, and not being able to get in touch with the Brigadier, Lieutenant-Colonel Tennant ordered the regiment to fall back and take up a position extending from the right flank of the 7th Dragoon Guards along the valley towards Square 17, where it was hoped contact would be made with the infantry.

This retirement was carried out in the nick of time, for shortly afterwards the enemy opened heavy artillery fire upon what had been the regiment's advanced position, and as no cover of any sort was available for either men or horses the casualties would have been extremely heavy. About midnight the enemy once more opened heavy artillery fire over the valley, but failed to locate the position, and the night passed without further incident except that a German patrol, advancing from Delville Wood, ran into one of the regimental listening patrols and was fired on, two prisoners being taken, both belonging to the 16th Bavarian Regiment. At 3.30 a.m. the Brigade was ordered to retire. Fortunately the morning was misty, which enabled the troops to ride back, undetected by the enemy, through the artillery positions (which were saturated with tear gas) to the valley of Montauban, where horses were watered and fed, and the Brigade returned to bivouac at Meaulte.

Later in the morning the Divisional Commander, Major-General Macandrew, visited the regiment and congratulated it on its performance, especially commending Captain Jarvis for his leading of the advanced guard.

The casualties were as follows:—Rissaldar Konsal Singh and Ressaidar Ali Sher Khan, wounded; 9 other ranks killed and 39 wounded (total 50); 19 horses killed and 53 wounded (total 72).

The Brigade remained in bivouac at Meaulte in a state of readiness to take instant advantage of any opportunity for breaking through the enemy line should such present itself, but on the evening of the 23rd returned to its former bivouac near Querrieu.

On the 29th July Lieutenant-Colonel Tennant proceeded on duty to England and Major Adams assumed command of the regiment.

On the 8th August the Brigade left Querrieu and marched to Airaines (via Daours, Amiens and Picquigny), where it halted for the night, continuing the march next day via Oisemont to Pierrecourt, in the valley of the River Bresle, where it went into billets.

On the 16th the Brigade moved to Riencourt and on the following day continued the march to Bussy les Daours, where it went into bivouac and furnished strong digging parties for the III Corps and XV Corps.

On the 20th the regiment moved to Pont Noyelles and on the 29th the whole Brigade moved to Molliens Vidame, continuing the march next day to Pierrecourt, where it went into billets.

On the 6th and 7th September the whole Division moved back to the Somme area, the later portion of the march being carried out by night so as to avoid the notice of the enemy's scouting planes, and it was not until 8.30 a.m. on the morning of the 8th September that the regiment reached its bivouac at Daours. Here it remained until the 13th, when a move was made to Meaulte. During the night of the 13th/14th September the Brigade marched to Mametz and remained there in a state of readiness. At 6.30 a.m. on the morning of the 15th September the infantry opened a big attack against the German line between Morval and Le Sars, and on this occasion tanks were used for the first time, causing a panic amongst the Germans. Flers was entered by a tank at 8.40 a.m., followed by the infantry, and the village was captured. High Wood, Martinpuich, and Courcelette were also captured. Hopes now ran high that the long-looked-for moment for mounted action had arrived and everyone anxiously awaited the order to advance. Had the enemy strongholds at Les Bœufs and Gueudecourt also been captured the whole of the 2nd Indian Cavalry Division would have advanced to exploit the success, but it was not to be and, once more disappointed, the Division retired, on the morning of the 17th, to its bivouac near Daours.

On the 26th September the regiment moved to Riencourt, continuing the march next day to Crouy, west of Amiens.

During the progress of the Somme battle the whole of the cavalry was once more formed into a Cavalry Corps under the command of General Kavanagh, and, in order to simplify the issue of orders, the 2nd (Indian) Cavalry Division now became the 5th Cavalry Division.

On the 1st November the Division moved into winter quarters west of Abbeville, the regiment being billeted on the area around Harcelaines.

During the month a Pioneer Battalion was created in each

Brigade, the Commanding Officer and Battalion Headquarters being furnished by each regiment in turn. The regimental Pioneer Company, under the command of Major Craster, included five British and five Indian Officers, and two hundred and fifty other ranks.

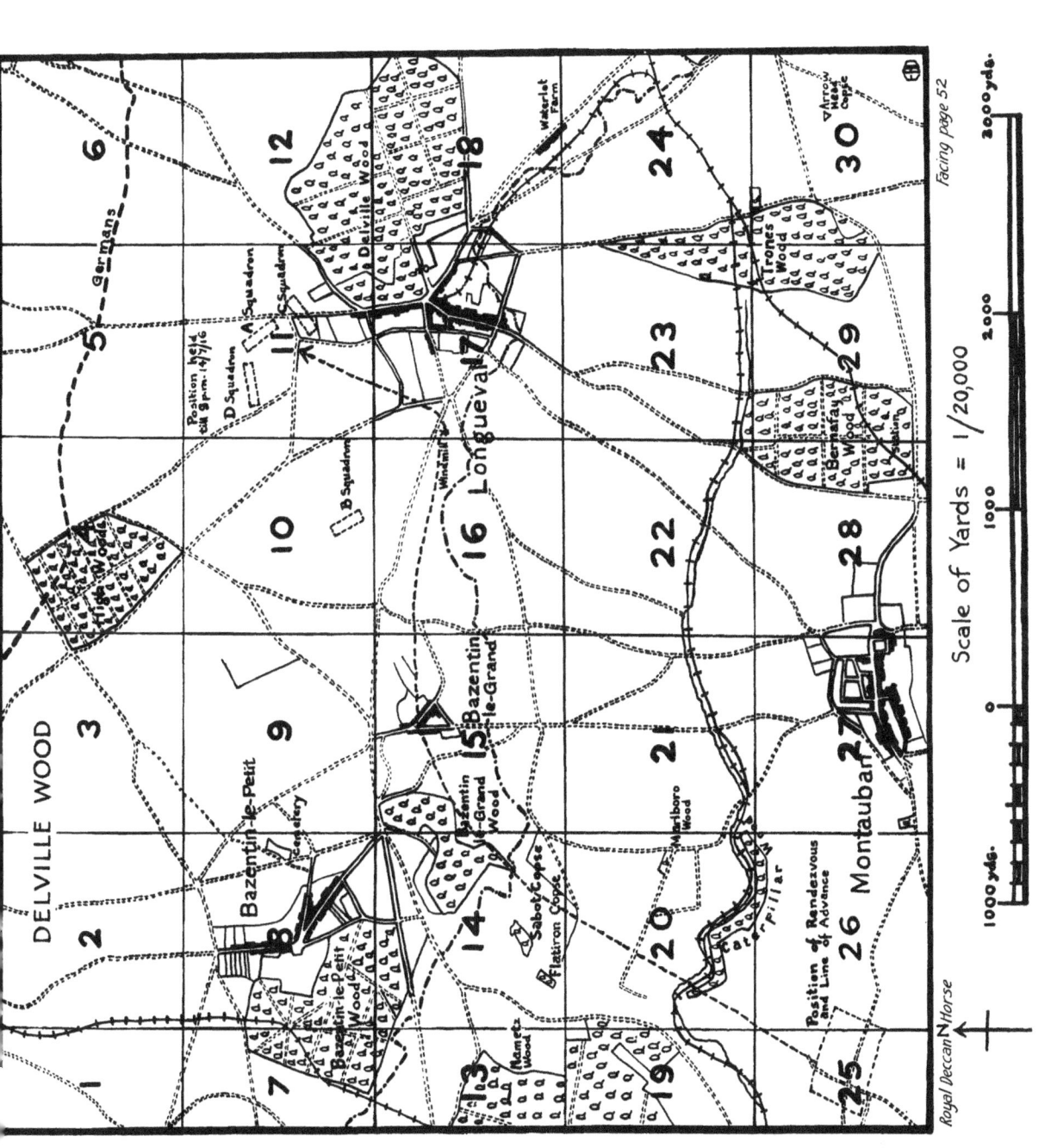

CHAPTER VII

1917

German Retirement—Trefcon—Raids by Second-Lieutenant Godfree and Captain Mulloy—Vadencourt Sector—Concentration for Passchendaele—Belgian Frontier—Cambrai—Gouzeaucourt.

THE regiment remained in billets at Harcelaines until the middle of March and was fortunate in being able to do so as the weather was generally bad, a considerable amount of frost and snow being experienced. Individual training and musketry were carried out whenever possible and the Pioneer Company was kept occupied in repairing roads, trenches, etc.

On the 14th March the Germans commenced a general retirement of their whole line, partly in order to reduce their length of front and partly in order to be better able to meet the French attack, under General Nivelle, regarding which no attempt at secrecy had been made. As the Germans retired they were followed up by the Allied forces along the whole front from the Roye road to the south of Arras.

On the 18th March the towns of Chaulnes and Bapaume were taken by our troops and on the following day Péronne and Mont St. Quentin were occupied.

On the 20th March the 5th Cavalry Division left its winter quarters and that evening the regiment arrived at Andainville. The march was continued on the next and following days via Hamel, Feuillères, Halle, Cléry and Curlu to Framerville, which was reached on the 30th. Here a halt was made until the 14th April. The whole of this march had been carried out under the most trying conditions. It rained or snowed practically every day and all day, in addition to which a cold, biting wind blew incessantly. Both men and horses had frequently to bivouac in mud and on one or two occasions this was so deep that the horses were standing up to their hocks in it.

On the 14th April the Brigade marched from Framerville to Trefcon, eight miles west of St. Quentin, through the country which had recently been evacuated by the Germans. This became known as the Devastated Area, and the amount of wilful damage that had been done was incredible. Fruit trees were cut through near the ground level, villages demolished, magnificent châteaux, famous in history, were reduced to heaps of stone, wells were fouled and poisoned and land mines were laid at every culvert and cross-road. The splendid library at Péronne, which contained many valuable French works, was utterly destroyed, and the whole countryside had been reduced to a dreary, desolate waste.

The Brigade remained at Trefcon for the next three months, one regiment at a time being detailed for duty in the front-line trenches, whilst the two remaining regiments were enabled to carry out mounted training over the open, devastated country. This was the first opportunity which had been afforded for such training since the regiment disembarked at Marseilles, with the exception of two short periods at St. Riquier in 1916.

On the 15th May it was the turn of the regiment to occupy the trenches, where they relieved the 2nd/5th Battalion The Leicestershire Regiment and continued to hold the line until the 14th June. The sector allotted to the regiment lay just in front of the village of Le Verguier and consisted of a number of small defensive posts (in trenches of from three to four feet deep), each containing a garrison, which varied in strength from one section to a complete troop, This line of posts was situated about 1,200 yards from the famous Hindenburg Line, which stretched from Vimy Ridge on the north as far as the St. Gobert Forest and the Chemin de Dames on the south. During its tour of duty the regiment greatly strengthened the existing posts, and patrols were employed nightly in wiring No Man's Land; and it is of interest to note that this particular portion of the line was enabled to hold out longer than any other sector during the great German offensive which took place the following March.

On the night of the 23rd May Second-Lieutenant Godfree, with a patrol, consisting of one duffadar and ten men, surprised a party of Germans, killing two and capturing three unwounded prisoners. The object of the raid was to reconnoitre the Ridge road with a view to ascertaining whether a suspected machine-gun emplacement existed in this locality. The patrol discovered the emplacement, which was surrounded by a few rifle pits, and as it was unoccupied the party concealed itself amongst some bushes by the side of the road and awaited events. At about 10 p.m. a solitary German soldier crept out from behind some trees, stopped to listen and, hearing nothing, lay down. He was shortly followed by five more men, who crawled into the rifle pits. Very soon afterwards two more Germans were seen to be moving directly towards the spot where the patrol lay concealed. Lieutenant Godfree, realizing that at any moment he might be discovered, made a dash with his patrol upon the enemy. A short scuffle ensued during which two Germans were killed and three were taken prisoners. The slight noise put the whole German line on the alert and immediately the entire area was brilliantly illuminated by Very lights and a heavy rifle fire was opened from the enemy trenches. The patrol at once scattered, to reassemble in some low ground to the rear, from whence it made its way back to the line, bringing its prisoners with it and without having suffered a single casualty. For this exploit Second-Lieutenant Godfree was subsequently awarded the Military Cross.

Another raid, on a larger scale, was carried out on the night of the 13th June by a composite squadron under Captain

Mulloy, supported by artillery and machine-gun fire. The object of this raid was to drive the enemy out of Ascension Wood. This was successfully accomplished, but on making its way back to our lines the squadron ran into a strong party of Germans and suffered several casualties. Amongst the killed was Lieutenant E. E. Lawford of the Indian Army Reserve of Officers, who had been attached to the regiment since July 1915. His loss was deeply deplored by all ranks. Five men were also killed and Lieutenant Glasspoole, Ressaidar Dalip Singh and twenty-two other ranks were wounded. Major Ross, D.S.O., who was serving on the staff as Brigade Major, was also wounded.

On the following day—the 14th—the Germans, in retaliation for the raid, opened a heavy bombardment upon our portion of the line and succeeded in obtaining a direct hit upon one of our posts which caused heavy casualties, five men being killed and six wounded. During the night the regiment was relieved by the Fort Garry Horse and returned to billets at Trefcon, where, on the 16th, the Brigade was inspected by the new Cavalry Corps Commander, General Kavanagh, who took occasion to compliment the regiment on its good work, referring especially to the brilliant leadership of the officers and the good fighting spirit of the men whilst in the front line.

On the 23rd June the regiment took over a fresh sector of the trench line known as the Vadencourt Sector, from the 18th Lancers, and remained in occupation until the 9th July, but nothing of especial interest took place.

On the 14th July—the anniversary of the attack on Delville Wood—the regiment commenced a long march from Trefcon northwards to Monchy Cayeux, in the vicinity of St. Pol, which was reached on the afternoon of the 20th, halts having been made at Cartigny, Suzanne, Morlancourt, Thièvres and Troisvaux. The whole of the Cavalry Corps was now concentrated in this neighbourhood in view of a possible break-through becoming feasible during the fresh offensive which was shortly to be launched upon Passchendaele.

On the 3rd August the following message from the G.O.C. III Corps was published :—

"I wish to put on record the excellent state of the defences in the area previously held by the Cavalry Corps and recently taken over by the 34th and 35th Divisions.

"If it is possible to pick out one formation, where the work of all was so good, I should mention the *5th Cavalry Division*. The obstacles put up by this Division are quite the best I have seen in this country."

And on the 9th August the following was received from the Military Secretary to the Commander-in-Chief to the G.O.C. Cavalry Corps :—

"The Commander-in-Chief directs me to convey to you and to all ranks of the Cavalry Corps his pleasure at the report received on the excellent state of the defences handed over by them. He considers that it reflects the greatest possible credit on all concerned and that the best traditions of the British Cavalry are being maintained."

On the 15th August a Divisional Horse Show was held in the grounds of a beautiful château at Bryas. Most of the events consisted of eliminating classes with a view to selecting representatives for the Division at the forthcoming Cavalry Corps Horse Show, which was held at Ramicourt Château on the 1st September. The latter was an unique occasion, as never before had there been such a gathering of cavalry regiments drawn from all quarters of the Empire; no fewer than twenty-six British, three Canadian, five Yeomanry and eleven Indian regiments being present.

On the 8th September the regiment was inspected by Lieutenant-General S. H. V. Cox, Military Secretary to the Secretary of State for India, and on the 16th the Cavalry Corps

Commander, Lieutenant-General Sir C. Kavanagh, presented the following decorations to officers, non-commissioned officers and men of the regiment :—

> Officier de l'Ordre de la Couronne : Lieutenant-Colonel F. Adams.
>
> Indian Distinguished Service Medal : Ressaidar Dalip Singh, Duffadar Mirza Muhammed Ali Beg.
>
> Indian Meritorious Service Medal : Kote-Duffadar Bheret Singh, Kote-Duffadar Abdul Razak Khan, Quartermaster Duffadar Sheikh Muhammed Ibrahim, Trumpet-Major Sheikh Zahur Muhammed, Acting Lance-Duffadar Lahri, and Sowar Sawai Singh.

On the 29th September Major R. B. Worgan, D.S.O. (who had been in command of an infantry regiment since 1915) was appointed to command the 173rd Infantry Brigade, with the temporary rank of Brigadier-General.

On the 6th October the regiment marched to Wittes and on the following day to Watou, in Belgium, where it remained in bivouac in a state of readiness. Owing, however, to the continuous heavy rain which now set in, the country beyond Ypres was converted into a veritable quagmire, difficult even for the infantry and quite impossible for cavalry, so that on the 15th October the regiment marched via Wardrecques and Fauquembergues to Royon and Loison, where it arrived on the 17th and went into billets. Here it remained for three weeks and then the whole Division was moved up in order to be able to take part in the forthcoming Battle of Cambrai.

On the 9th November the regiment, in brigade, made a long march of thirty-nine miles to Boisbergues; on the 10th it reached Contay, and the next day Froiss, arriving at Mametz late on the evening of the 12th November. During the night of the 19th/20th the whole Division was moved to a position of readiness at Bois Dessarte, north-east of Fins, where it arrived at 5 a.m. on the 20th and remained concealed under cover. This was the opening day of the Battle of Cambrai and patrols were pushed forward to keep touch with the infantry with a view to the Division passing through the enemy's line should opportunity offer, raiding his communications, disorganizing his system of command, damaging the railways and interfering with the arrival of reinforcements.

The attack opened at 6.20 a.m. with the tanks advancing over a six-mile front, from Gonnelieu to beyond Heudicourt. Our infantry passed through the Hindenburg Line and drove the enemy out of their shelters and dug-outs, and the prospect of a cavalry break-through seemed most hopeful. About noon the 5th Cavalry Division advanced, the Secunderabad Cavalry Brigade moving to Marcoing, whence a report had been received that our infantry had captured the bridge-head over the St. Quentin Canal. Marcoing was reached about 2.15 p.m. after a march of nearly eight miles over a very complicated system of trenches. As the village was in the possession of our infantry the Brigade pushed forward to the canal. Whilst crossing the bridge, however, the 7th Dragoon Guards at once came under very heavy machine-gun fire and it soon became clear that the Marcoing–Masnières–Beaurevoir line was still held by unbroken German infantry and that our own infantry had not yet reached their final objective, which would have opened the way for the cavalry. As the Divisional Commander's orders were most explicit that the Cavalry Brigade must on no account be drawn into the infantry fight and that the work of the cavalry did not commence until the infantry had secured their final objective, the further advance of the Brigade was held up and once more hopes were dashed to the ground, just when success seemed to be within its grasp.

The Brigade remained in a position of readiness throughout the remainder of the day and for the whole of the 21st, but on the 22nd, all hope having been abandoned, it returned to Fins. From Fins the march was continued the next day to Mericourt-sur-Somme where a halt was made for a couple of days, and on the 27th it returned to its old quarters at Trefcon.

On the morning of the 30th November the Germans opened an attack over a ten-mile front from Vendhuille to Masnières, and things did not go too well for us. The Secunderabad Cavalry Brigade was immediately moved up through Villers Faucon to a valley about one mile south-west of Gouzeaucourt, where it arrived about 3 p.m. The position had now become serious. The Germans had already captured Villers Guislain, Gonnelieu, Bonaris and Gouzeaucourt, and were menacing La Vacquerie, in addition to which a large number of our guns had fallen into their hands. At this juncture the Guards were sent forward to counter-attack just west of Gouzeaucourt and the 5th Cavalry Division was moved up in support. The German advance having been stemmed, the horses were sent to the rear and the Secunderabad Cavalry Brigade was ordered to relieve the Guards Brigade and took over the front trench-line in the following order: Hodson's Horse on the right, XXth Deccan Horse in the centre and Poona Horse on the left.

At about 4 p.m. the Germans, under cover of a heavy barrage, renewed the attack, but were everywhere repulsed, our troops in the front line having taken the precaution to move forward directly the barrage commenced. The regiment continued to hold this line till the night of the 2nd/3rd December, when it was relieved by the 18th Hussars and marched back to Heudicourt (where the horses had been left), and then moved with the remainder of the Brigade to a position near Saulcourt.

During the period it was in the trenches the regiment lost two men killed and ten wounded from enemy artillery fire. Captain Mulloy, M.C., attached to the regiment, and the French interpreter, M. Azemar, were wounded, the latter subsequently dying from his injuries.

During the remainder of the month of December the regiment provided strong digging parties for work on the Corps reserve trenches and for wiring No Man's Land in front of our line.

CHAPTER VIII

1st January 1918 to 15th August 1918

Indian Cavalry ordered to Palestine—Embarkation at Marseilles—Arrival at Alexandria—Advance to Belah—Formation of 14th Cavalry Brigade and 5th Cavalry Division—Situation in Palestine—Desert Mounted Corps—Jordan Valley—Issue of Lances—El Ghoraniye.

THE outlook for the cavalry at the opening of the new year was decidedly not cheerful. The great offensive at Passchendaele had not yielded the full success anticipated (mainly on account of the atrocious weather conditions), and the Germans had retired to the strongly fortified Hindenburg Line, from which they would have to be driven before mounted action could become possible. In these circumstances it was decided to reduce the number of mounted troops in France and utilize their services in another theatre of the war where they would have more scope. Accordingly General Allenby, the Commander-in-Chief of the Army in Palestine, had been informed that the whole of the Indian Cavalry in France would be despatched shortly and placed at his disposal.

Throughout January and the greater part of February the regiment continued to furnish strong working parties for strengthening the lines in the vicinity of Vendelles and Pœuilly, with a break of one week (25th to 30th January) when they took a turn of trench duty, relieving the 18th Hussars, in the vicinity of Vadencourt.

Regimental Headquarters, together with all horses and transport, left Trefcon on the 1st February and marched, via Weincourt, to St. Ouen (where the remainder of the regiment joined them on the 17th).

On the 9th February orders were received for the Brigade to proceed to Egypt, and on the same day Rissaldar-Major Prem Singh Bahadur and Rissaldar Khurshed Khan left for England to attend the ceremony of the opening of Parliament.

On the 28th February the regiment left St. Ouen and marched, via Cottenchy and Prouzel, to Neuville, where it remained for a fortnight to enable the establishment, both in men and horses, to be brought up to full strength.

On the 19th and 20th March the regiment entrained at Saleux for Marseilles, where, on arrival on the 22nd, it went into camp at La Valentine and Mont Furou.

On the eve of the departure of the Indian Cavalry the Field-Marshal Commander-in-Chief issued the following communiqué :—

"As the Indian Cavalry are now leaving France I wish to record my great appreciation of the valour, determination and devotion to duty shown by all ranks in the field. Indian Officers, N.C.Os. and men have been absent for more than three years in a foreign country, thousands of miles from their homes and families, in a climate to which they are totally unaccustomed, and have, by their gallant deeds added even greater lustre to the already glorious names of their respective regiments."

On the 30th March the regiment embarked on the Hired Transports *Pancras* and *Menominee* and sailed on the 1st April. Malta was reached on the 4th and here the *Menominee* had to remain for some days to enable certain repairs to her engines to be carried out. The *Pancras* arrived at Alexandria on the 10th April and, as soon as disembarked, the troops were railed to Tel el Kebir, where they arrived late at night and went into camp. An opportunity was now taken to grant leave to as many Indian Officers and men as could be spared, and on the 13th two Indian Officers and forty-five other ranks proceeded on leave to India.

On the 16th April the portion of the regiment under Captain Tinley, which had been detained at Malta, rejoined, and on the 22nd the XXth Deccan Horse and the 34th Poona Horse (all that was left of the old Secunderabad Cavalry Brigade) marched through a terrific sandstorm to Kantara (via Kassassin, Ismailia and El Ferdan), where a couple of days were spent, and on the 27th entrained for Belah, which was reached on the 28th.

The XXth Deccan Horse, together with the Poona Horse, the Sherwood Rangers, 20th Machine Gun Squadron and a Signal Troop, Royal Engineers, formed the 7th Mounted Brigade, under the command of Brigadier-General C. V. Clarke, D.S.O., and, together with two other brigades, constituted the 2nd Mounted Division under Major-General Macandrew. These titles were subsequently changed to 14th Cavalry Brigade and 5th Cavalry Division and the whole of the mounted troops in Palestine were formed into a Corps, entitled the Desert Mounted Corps, under the command of Lieutenant-General Sir H. G. Chauvel. This Corps consisted of the 4th Cavalry Division, the 5th Cavalry Division, the Australian and New Zealand Mounted Division, and the Australian Mounted Division.

The regiment remained at Belah until the 4th May and then marched, via Gaza, El Mejdal, Khurbet Sukereir and Ayumkara, to a camp on the seashore near Sarona, which was reached on the 7th, and spent the next two months in training.

On the 15th June Lieutenant-Colonel Adams was awarded the Distinguished Service Order.

On the 27th June the Brigade was inspected by the Commander-in-Chief, General Allenby, and shortly after midnight on the 28th/29th June it left Sarona and marched, via Ramleh, to Lahron. Enab was reached on the following day and on the 1st July the march was continued, via Jerusalem, to Jericho, where the Brigade arrived about midnight on the 2nd/3rd July. Up till now the weather had been relatively cool, but from the beginning of July it grew steadily hotter.

On the 8th the Brigade left Jericho to take its turn in holding the bridge-head over the Jordan at El Ghoraniye.

The situation in Palestine at this period was, briefly, as follows :—

The Turkish forces (32,000 rifles, 4,000 sabres and 400 guns), under the Supreme Command of Marshal Liman von Sanders, were divided by the River Jordan into two separate bodies : the Seventh and Eighth Armies holding the line west of the river, and the Fourth Army that on the east, with Headquarters at Nazareth.

The Turkish line extended from Arsuf on the Mediterranean (with advance rail-head at Jil Julie) through Mesha, Furka and El Lubban down to the Jordan at Umm-el-Shert, thence across the river through Es Salt to Amman on the Hedjaz railway.

The main line of communication for the western portion was the railway from Jil Julie through Tul Keram to Afule and thence, via Beisan, to Deraa, where it joined the Hedjaz main line.

The forces east of the Jordan were entirely dependent upon the Hedjaz line.

For lateral communication there was a metalled road, running roughly parallel with the railway, from Jil Julie to Nablus, but from the latter place only two bad mountain tracks led down to the Jordan Valley at El Makhruk, whence the river was crossed by a single track leading, through very broken and difficult country, to Jisr el Damieh and Es Salt, so that the Turkish forces east of the river were practically isolated from those on the west.

Our own force totalled some 57,000 rifles, 12,000 sabres and 540 guns.

The mounted troops (The Desert Mounted Corps) under the command of Lieutenant-General Sir H. Chauvel, consisted of the following regiments: 5 Territorial Yeomanry, 15 Australian Light Horse, 3 New Zealand Mounted Rifles, 12 Indian Cavalry, 3 Indian Imperial Service Cavalry and 1 Chasseurs d'Afrique (French).

Before resuming the narrative it will be as well to give a short description of the Jordan Valley.

The River Jordan flows through a deep trough in a wild, mountainous and desolate region, the river bed at El Ghoraniye being some 1,200 feet below the level of the sea. The width of the Valley varies from a quarter to two miles, the bottom being covered with dense, rank undergrowth. Normally, the river is between forty and fifty yards wide, but it is deep and swift and liable to rapid rises after heavy rain. In the entire distance between the Lake of Tiberias and the Dead Sea (seventy-five miles) there are only six fordable places.

The mountains on either side rise abruptly in precipices from the river, some 3,000 feet below.

The road from Jerusalem to El Ghoraniye (twenty-two miles) descends by an easy gradient for the first nine or ten miles and then falls abruptly through narrow, rocky defiles with precipitous sides and hairpin turns, until it debouches upon the river bed.

The heat in the Valley during the summer months is intense, the thermometer averaging 115° and often rising as high as 130° and, in addition, the atmosphere, owing to the enormous evaporation from the Dead Sea, is laden with moisture. Furthermore, the increased air pressure, due to the depth below sea-level, creates a feeling of exhaustion, so much so that after a period of duty of less than a month's duration even the horses became so weary that they had to be coaxed to drag themselves along for a distance of a couple of miles to be watered. To add to the horrors of the place the valley is infested with mosquitos, causing malaria of a most virulent type. Evacuations to hospital from this cause alone amounted to thirty per cent. of the force each month. Indeed, the conditions are so bad that even the native Arabs are obliged to evacuate the valley during the summer months.

After perusing this brief description the reader may wonder why the Commander-in-Chief decided that it was imperative to hold this pestiferous valley during the summer months.

In the first place the retention of the bridge-heads at El Ghoraniye and Hajlah made the right flank of the army secure, and as, before the next advance commenced, we should require to be in possession of the valley and river crossings, it was considered to be less costly in the long run to continue to hold these than to abandon them to the enemy in the summer and then be obliged to retake them later on. Also, the River Jordan was the only dependable source from which drinking water could be obtained.

Secondly, the enemy Fourth Army, on the eastern side of the river, was prevented from obtaining supplies from vessels crossing the Dead Sea and was thus entirely dependent upon the Hedjaz railway, traffic over which was being constantly interrupted by Lawrence's Arab levies.

But the reason which probably carried the most weight was the fact that Marshal Liman von Sanders appeared to be firmly convinced that our next advance would be made on the east side of the Jordan, and therefore it was of the utmost importance that nothing should be done which might shake him in this opinion.

The defence of the Valley was divided into two sectors:—

(1) The north bank of the Wadi Aujah up to its junction with the Jordan, including the bridge-head there.

(2) From the Aujah bridge-head (exclusive) along the west bank of the Jordan as far as the Dead Sea, including the bridges and bridge-head at El Ghoraniye. This latter was the sector in which the regiment was employed.

Each sector was held by a strong force of infantry to which were attached three squadrons of cavalry for reconnaissance duties.

Roughly, the defence line of the second sector lay along the perimeter of a semi-circle the diameter of which was formed by the Jordan.

Gateways were left at intervals through the barbed wire to enable mounted patrols to pass in and out.

During daylight the cavalry relied upon Cossack posts, each a troop strong, but these were replaced at nightfall by a regular system of outposts.

The portion of the perimeter allotted to the regiment extended from the left of the line for a distance of about two miles. On their right came the Poona Horse, and the Sherwood Rangers carried the line back to the river.

Encounters between our patrols and parties of the enemy were of almost daily occurrence and afforded much experience to all ranks. Our tactics were the same as those which had invariably proved successful in France, viz.: to charge at the gallop, no matter what disparity of force there might be. It was found, however, that although the new-pattern thrusting sword is a first-class weapon for use against a mounted enemy, it is not equally effective (when moving fast over rough ground) against a dismounted man who lies in a ditch or takes cover behind a boulder. To overcome this disadvantage Colonel Adams issued instructions for patrols to collect and bring in any lances they found, of which there were several scattered about the country. As soon as a sufficient quantity had been obtained, our patrols were armed with them, with such good results that a Turkish prisoner was reported to have stated that even intending deserters were afraid to leave their lines for fear that they would be "stuck" before being able to explain their intention!

Upon these facts being brought to the notice of the Commander-in-Chief he issued orders that henceforth the whole of the Indian cavalry were to be armed with lances, and this was carried out prior to the commencement of the great advance in October. This is of especial interest as, since the War, the Army Council has decided that the lance is obsolete and is only to be used on ceremonial occasions!

Nothing of note occurred until the morning of the 10th July, when a small party of German troops made a surprise attack upon No. 1 Piquet Post, just before dawn. The piquet commander was obliged to fall back for some little distance in order to avoid being cut off, but as soon as he reached a defensible position, he halted his piquet and opened fire, whereupon the enemy retired.

In the meantime, Captain Larkin, the squadron commander, alarmed by the sound of firing, had ridden forward, accompanied by Lieutenant Heaton-Armstrong and a couple of orderlies, towards No. 1 Piquet Post to ascertain what had happened.

Suddenly, and without warning, the party was fired upon at short range and all four horses were shot. Captain Larkin and one of the orderlies were taken prisoner and the other orderly was killed. Lieutenant Heaton-Armstrong, although severely wounded in the neck and leg, doubled down a wadi, in which some bushes covered him, and, on reaching our lines, raised the alarm.

Captain Tinley, who was in command of the reserve squadron at Brigade Headquarters, was immediately despatched with his squadron to endeavour to rescue Captain Larkin and the orderly, but owing to the thickness of the scrub, the broken nature of the ground and ignorance of the direction taken by the enemy, his efforts were unavailing.

Captain Larkin's loss was greatly regretted. He came to the regiment from the Glasgow Yeomanry in April 1915 and immediately identified himself wholeheartedly with it; so much so that he had recently relinquished his rank of captain in the Yeomanry in order to obtain a transfer to the establishment of the Indian Army, and at the time of his capture he was in command of "B" Squadron.

The regiment remained on outpost duty at the Ghoraniye bridge-head until the morning of the 15th July, when it returned to the standing camp on the west side of the river. During its tour of duty it had captured seventeen prisoners and one horse and suffered the following casualties: Captain Larkin, taken prisoner; Lieutenant Heaton-Armstrong, severely wounded; other ranks, killed or missing 8, wounded 5; horses, killed (or missing) 17.

CHAPTER IX

15TH AUGUST 1918 TO 30TH SEPTEMBER 1918

Plan for General Advance—Description of Country—Concentration of Mounted Troops—The Advance—Carmel Range—Afule—Athlit—March to Damascus—Kiswe—Ashrafie—Fall of Damascus.

THE time was now drawing near for the final advance, the general plan for which was as follows :—

An overwhelming force of infantry and guns, together with three divisions of cavalry, was to be concentrated in the coastal sector. At zero hour the XXI Corps, supported by the heavy artillery, was to make a general attack on the Turkish position from Jil Julie to the sea and, having driven the enemy back from their defensive lines, was to wheel to the right, pivoting on Jil Julie, and push the enemy's right wing back into the hills. Through the open gap thus formed between Jil Julie and the sea the three cavalry divisions were to dash, advance along the coastal plain, cross the Carmel range by the Musmas Pass and, after debouching upon the plain of Esdraelon, take the railway junction at Afule and, proceeding via the Valley of Jezreel to Beisan, cut the railway at that place and then occupy the bridge over the Jordan at Jisr el Hussein. This having been accomplished, the port of Haifa was to be occupied. At the same time the Arab forces east of the Jordan were to cut the Hedjaz railway at Deraa.

In order to keep the enemy's Seventh and Eighth Armies pinned to their positions for a sufficient time to enable the above programme to be carried out, the XX Corps was to make a general attack against the rest of the line, and another force, advancing up the Jordan Valley, was to seize the bridge at El Damieh. The Seventh and Eighth Turkish Armies would then be penned in between the sea on their right and the Jordan on their left, with all their communications cut. Furthermore, the Fourth Army would be isolated, and, if the Arabs succeeded in taking Deraa, its communications would also be cut.

For the success of this plan it was essential that the concentration of the troops in the coastal area should be kept unknown to the enemy. To this end a series of demonstrations were carried out in the Jordan Valley with the object of confirming the views of the Turks that an advance east of the Jordan was intended. All movements of troops *eastwards* were carried out by *day* and, in order to add to the deception, huge clouds of dust were raised in the vicinity of Jericho by dragging rough sledges, drawn by mules, along the tracks. On the other hand, all marches by troops assigned to the coastal sector were carried out by night. Tents were left standing in the abandoned camps and additional ones pitched. Even dummy horses and mules were set up in the horse lines with a view to making it appear that reinforcements had arrived in that area.

The plan for the advance of the mounted troops was roughly as follows :—

As soon as the infantry had forced a passage, the three cavalry divisions were to advance rapidly northwards; the 5th Division by the coastal road through Mukhalid and the remainder via Tabsor and Mughair. No serious opposition was expected until the line of the Nahr el Mefjir was reached, where it was known that the enemy had a defensive line. The 5th Division was allotted the task of forcing this line between Liktera and the mouth of the river. Then the whole force was to change direction and move north-east towards the Carmel range, the 5th Division crossing by the track from Sindiane to Abu Shusheh and the remainder by the famous Musmas

Pass. Upon reaching the Plain of Esdraelon, on the far side of the mountains, the 5th Division was to advance upon Nazareth, capture the enemy's General Headquarters at that place (and, if possible, Marshal Liman von Sanders himself) and then clear the plain as far as Afule; to the 4th Division was allotted the task of capturing Beisan and cutting the railway there and also of seizing the bridge over the Jordan at Jisr el Hussein. The Australian Mounted Division, moving in rear of the 4th Division, was to march from El Lejjun to Jenin and thus block the road for the Turks retiring from Nablus through the Dothan Pass.

The district near the coast consists of a narrow strip of seashore not more than ten yards wide, from which steep sand dunes rise abruptly to a height of one hundred feet or so, on to a sandy plain varying from five to seven miles wide and covered with dunes of loose, shifting sand and a rank growth of coarse grass. This coastal plain extends northwards for a distance of some fifty miles and then comes to an abrupt end against the Carmel range of mountains which run down to the sea coast, ending in steep cliffs. The only track over the Carmel range at all possible for wheeled traffic is via the Musmas Pass from Kerkur to El Lejjun where it debouches upon the Plain of Esdraelon. The Musmas is a narrow, rocky defile, so shut in by precipitous cliffs that a comparatively small force could hold it for an indefinite time against a very considerable army. The route from Sindiane to Abu Shusheh is nothing but a goat track, quite impossible for wheeled traffic.

On the evening of the 15th August the Brigade moved to Talaat ed Dumm. Here it lay concealed during the 16th and marched on that and the following nights to a camp at Khirbet Deiran. Here a halt was made and the next four weeks were occupied in training and preparing for the approaching offensive.

On the evening of the 16th September the regiment, together with the remainder of the 5th Cavalry Division, marched during the night from Khirbet Deiran to Summeil, near Sarona, where there were extensive orange groves. These orange groves were of inestimable value, not only in providing complete concealment from observation, but also on account of the small irrigation canals which flowed through them, thereby enabling the horses to be watered without coming out of cover.

On the night of the 18th/19th September the Desert Mounted Corps moved to an assembly position on the seashore, some three-quarters of a mile north-west of El Jelil.

At 4.30 a.m. (zero hour) on the 19th September the artillery opened fire upon the Turkish positions and five infantry divisions moved forward simultaneously for the attack.

The Turks were completely surprised and in a little over an hour the whole of their positions were in our hands and the wheel to the right commenced.

The 5th Cavalry Division, following close behind the infantry, was soon well away, and by noon had reached the Nahr el Mefjir, where horses were watered and fed. Practically no resistance had been met with and the small Turkish garrison at Liktera surrendered upon demand.

Patrols were now despatched to obtain information regarding the Sindiane track across the mountains, concerning which very little was known. They reported that it was totally unfit for wheeled traffic and consequently the transport of the 5th Division was directed to cross by the Musmas Pass in rear of that of the 4th Division. It should here be mentioned that, in order to increase mobility, all transport had been reduced to a minimum. Each man carried three days' rations for himself (including the "iron" ration) and two nosebags (containing $8\frac{1}{2}$ lb. of grain each) for his horse. A third day's forage was carried on G.S. wagons (three per regiment), but these did not accompany the

Division, but followed some distance in rear and acted as a mobile depot.

All entrenching tools were carried on pack animals. The only vehicles which accompanied the Divisions were those carrying ammunition and the light motor ambulances.

When their rations were consumed the force would have to rely upon the country for more.

The 5th Division resumed its march at 6 p.m., but it was long after dark before it reached Sindiane. Up to this point the advance had been made over loose sand, which was very heavy going and most trying to the horses, but now the hilly country was reached and the passage over the Carmel range had to be carried out over rough and narrow mountain paths, little better than goat tracks. Speed being vital, the advance was made at a steady pace and not by a system of bounds, with the consequence that the troops in the rear of the column had the utmost difficulty in maintaining touch with the units in front. At one period, where the track became more than usually narrow and difficult, connecting files between units stretched out over a distance of three miles. This rapid advance, however, prevented the enemy from arriving in time to bar the route, and the mountains were crossed without opposition, the village of Abu Shusheh being occupied by 2.30 a.m. on the morning of the 20th September. The distance covered in the first twenty-four hours was, roughly, sixty miles.

A short halt was made at Abu Shusheh to enable the units in rear to close up, and then the advance was continued (fortunately the moon was nearly full and the light good) to Warakani, where the Afule—Haifa railway line was cut. On reaching Junjar, at the foot of the Nazareth hills, the 14th Brigade halted until daylight and then " C " Squadron, under Captain Tinley, was sent forward to sweep up parties of the enemy who were observed in the neighbourhood of the village of Afule.

As the squadron advanced fire was opened upon it from a wadi on its flank, some two hundred yards distant. A troop was immediately despatched at a gallop against the enemy, who thereupon promptly surrendered and the whole party, consisting of two officers and thirty other ranks, were taken prisoner. Captain Tinley now advanced with his squadron towards the railway station of Afule and opened an attack upon it. The defenders, taken by surprise and being thoroughly demoralized, offered a very feeble resistance and the railway station was speedily captured, together with two officers (both Germans) and a hundred and twenty other ranks. In the village more parties of the enemy were rounded up and the Squadron then returned to the regiment, bringing back two hundred and ninety-six prisoners, including five officers (three of whom were Germans) and five German non-commissioned officers.

Very shortly after " C " Squadron had been despatched, Ressaidar Bachant Singh of " A " Squadron was ordered to take his troop in a south-easterly direction and deal with any enemy parties with whom he might come in contact. He returned at about 11 a.m. bringing two hundred and seventy-six prisoners (including five Officers) and some hundred animals, making a total of five hundred and eighty-two prisoners captured (including ten Officers), a hundred animals and the Field Cashier's lorry.

The outstanding feature of the day's operations was the demonstration of the fact that small bodies of cavalry can successfully dispose of almost any number of enemy troops when surprise is on the side of the attackers and the morale of the enemy is weak. In the one case a troop disposed of ten times its own numbers, and in the other a weak squadron (the strength at the time was less than fifty sabres) captured Afule station and brought back nearly three hundred prisoners. There is no doubt that the enemy was thoroughly demoralized by our rapid and unexpected advance and in no case offered more than a half-hearted resistance.

Shortly after midday the whole regiment moved up close to Afule station and remained there for the night.

At three o'clock on the morning of the 23rd the 5th Division marched upon Haifa, but the regiment was allotted no active part in the operations which resulted in the capture of that place, and bivouacked on the seashore just east of Haifa.

On the morning of the 24th September, information having been received that our cars and lorries, moving along the coastal road from Tantara to Haifa, were being fired upon from Athlit, and as it was necessary not only to put a stop to this as soon as possible, but also to gain touch with the Hyderabad Imperial Service Lancers advancing upon Tantara, a detached force, under the command of Colonel Adams, consisting of the XXth Deccan Horse, one section Royal Horse Artillery and two armoured cars, was ordered to clear up the situation at Athlit, an old stronghold of the Crusaders, situated on the sea coast about ten miles south of Haifa.

Athlit was reached at 1 p.m. and found to be devoid of enemy troops, but forty rifles were collected there. The advance was then resumed and Tantara reached at about 3 p.m. Here touch was gained with an advance patrol of the Hyderabad Lancers, and at Shefeia, a few miles further on, contact having been obtained with the main body of the regiment, the detachment returned to camp, having covered a distance of about thirty miles.

By this time the whole of the Turkish Seventh and Eighth Armies had been either captured or killed and all their guns, stores and transport had fallen into our hands. The Fourth Army, east of the Jordan, was retreating upon Damascus and the Commander-in-Chief determined to cut it off and capture this well-known and important city also. Accordingly the

Desert Mounted Corps received orders to advance upon Damascus.

Two brigades of the Australian Mounted Division were directed to advance over the foothills on the western side of Damascus in order to block the roads leading to Homs and Beirut. The G.O.C. 5th Division received orders to send one brigade round the eastern side of the city (to gain touch with the Australians on the Homs road) and to place the remainder of his Division astride the Deraa–Damascus road at or near Kiswe in order " to receive the remnants of the Turkish Fourth Army which was to be driven into their welcoming arms by the 4th Division."*

At dawn on the 26th September the regiment, in brigade, marched to Kefr Kenna, where it arrived at about 6 p.m. on the same day. Here a halt was made until two o'clock in the morning (the 27th) and the march was then resumed to Tiberias, on the western shore of the lake of that name, which was entered at 7.30 a.m. After watering and feeding, the advance was continued at noon and Kusr Atra, on the southern end of Lake Huleh, was reached by six o'clock in the evening (the 27th). Here a halt was made for the night and at 4 p.m. on the following afternoon (the 28th) the regiment marched to El Kuneitra, arriving at ten o'clock in the morning and halting until 5.30 p.m., when the advance upon Damascus was resumed. (It is worthy of mention that throughout this advance and up to the end of the War the entire Corps was dependent upon local resources for subsistence for both men and horses.)

On the morning of the 30th, when the Corps was still a few miles short of Sasa, information was received that the leading portion of the Turkish Fourth Army, retreating upon Damascus, was approaching Kiswe via the old Pilgrims' Road.

* *Desert Mounted Corps*, p. 266.

Facing page 78

PALESTINE – 1st Phase

Royal Deccan Horse

Orders were at once issued for the 13th and 14th Brigades to intercept this force.

The 14th Brigade advanced at great speed (though the pace was frequently checked by having to pass through fields of standing maize), along the north bank of the Wadi es Zabirani towards Kiswe, where the Pilgrims' Road crosses the river, about nine miles south of Damascus. As the Brigade approached Kiswe, patrols reported the village to be strongly held and that the enemy were established on the hills of El Jebel el Aswad, lying to the north. They further reported that the Pilgrims' Road was packed with troops and transport of all descriptions.

At about 9 a.m. enemy snipers opened fire on the column from some hills just south of Sasa, and Lieutenant Foa was detached with a troop to deal with the situation, with the result that seven of the enemy were killed and the troop then returned to the regiment. After crossing the Wadi es Zabirani at about 10 a.m., "A" Squadron, under Major Jarvis, M.C., was sent out in a north-easterly direction towards the Pilgrims' Road (Damascus-es-Sanamain) to ascertain the whereabouts of the enemy retiring along it. No signs of the enemy were met with until the Squadron got to within three-quarters of a mile north of Kiswe, from which point hostile troops were seen marching along the road, and some three hundred infantry moved out from the village and opened machine-gun and rifle fire on the Squadron. At the same time large bodies of enemy troops were observed south of Kiswe, marching north. Major Jarvis took up a dismounted position on the east of Jebel el Mania, covering the road, and opened fire on the enemy moving along it. A motor-car advancing towards Kiswe was captured and also two Officers and sixty-eight other ranks, who were handed over to the Australian Mounted Division, which was moving round west of Damascus. Meanwhile "C" Squadron, under Captain Tinley, which was acting as advanced guard to the Brigade, pushed forward and, after capturing some thirty enemy, occupied a height overlooking the road and to the north of "A" Squadron, and opened fire upon the enemy troops on the main road. The Turks, however, brought up a weak battalion of infantry and, covered by some ten mountain guns, commenced a counter-attack. "C" Squadron held its ground until the enemy had approached to within forty yards and was then obliged to fall back. At this juncture the remainder of the regiment arrived and "D" Squadron was detached to seize a height to the north-west, whilst "B" Squadron pushed forward on to the hill from which "C" Squadron had retired, and the Turks, seeing themselves almost surrounded, hastily retreated in the direction of Kiswe. The Turkish main forces on the Pilgrims' Road were now visible marching in a northerly direction, followed by the troops who had been driven out of Kiswe; consequently the Brigade resumed its advance towards Damascus.

At about 3 p.m. "B" and "C" Squadrons, under Lieutenant Godfree and Captain Tinley respectively, received orders to seize a conical hill near the village of Ashrafie, which was seen to be occupied by the enemy. This hill was galloped and the enemy driven off, but shortly afterwards the Turks opened machine-gun fire from some plantations situated to the north of the village and "B" Squadron was sent forward to drive them out. The shortest route lay through the village, upon entering which the Headquarters of an entire Turkish cavalry regiment, comprising thirty-four Officers, a hundred and sixty-eight other ranks and two machine guns, together with a Cavalry Divisional Commander, surrendered and were left in the charge of one troop, whilst the remainder of the squadron pushed forward to its objective. The plantations were captured at about 5 p.m., together with twenty-one Turks and two machine guns, and then Lieutenant Godfree, with one squadron, rode on and entered Damascus itself, near the Kadem station.

At this juncture, however, Captain Tinley, the senior Officer on the spot, received peremptory orders not to enter Damascus (notwithstanding that there was no serious opposition) and accordingly he directed Lieutenant Godfree to withdraw his squadron. On the following day, the 1st October, the honour of leading the way into Damascus was assigned to the Arab army under Lawrence, but this does not alter the fact that " B " Squadron entered Damascus proper at about 5 p.m. on the evening of the 30th September.

The total number of prisoners captured by the regiment during the day (the 30th September) amounted to: 36 Officers (including one Cavalry Divisional General), 294 other ranks (including 26 Germans), 200 horses and mules, 4 machine guns, 1 motor-car.

The casualties suffered were: 1 British Officer (Lieutenant Hallifax), wounded; 1 Indian Officer (Ressaidar Dalip Singh, I.D.S.M.), died of wounds; 3 Indian other ranks, killed; 10 Indian other ranks, wounded.

CHAPTER X

1ST OCTOBER 1918 TO 31ST DECEMBER 1918

Advance to Homs—Lure of Aleppo—Advance of 5th Cavalry Division from Homs—Fall of Aleppo—Armistice—Record of 5th Cavalry Division—Lessons from the Campaign.

DAMASCUS was occupied on the morning of the 1st October and on the 2nd October the Corps Commander, at the head of the 4th and 5th Cavalry Divisions, made his state entry through the city. The regiment bivouacked that night at El Judeide, south-west of the city.

On the 3rd October Sowar Abdul Ghani Khan, who had been taken prisoner by the Turks when acting as orderly to Captain Larkin at the bridge-head at El Ghoraniye, rejoined the regiment, having escaped on the fall of Damascus.

Men and horses were now given a very necessary rest, for in the past twelve days they had covered over two hundred miles and fought several actions. The long marches at a rapid pace on short rations had made the horses very thin and tired, and large numbers of men were down with malaria and influenza. It was considered so essential, however, to cut the railway line at Rayak and capture the port of Beirut that on the 5th October the 4th and 5th Divisions were once more on the march, the 4th Division being directed upon Beirut, which was taken without opposition, and the 5th Division upon Rayak, through Shtora. During its advance the 5th Division captured 177 prisoners and some guns at Zahli and entered Rayak on the afternoon of the 6th October.

The Commander-in-Chief now decided upon making a further advance as far as Homs, but the 4th and Australian

Divisions were so depleted by sickness as to be unfit for further action and the task therefore fell upon the 5th Division, which was also far below strength, the total number of sabres being not more than 1,500, and squadrons were lucky if they could muster sixty sabres. No opposition was encountered and Homs was occupied on the 15th October.

Homs itself was a place of no importance—the goal lay many miles ahead, viz., Aleppo, the political and strategical values of which were immense. If we could seize it we should be astride the main railway line leading to Constantinople and consequently the whole of the Arab territory as far as the Euphrates would fall into our hands. Aleppo lies more than one hundred miles north of Homs and no reinforcements could be hastily sent forward, the railway bridge at Hama having been destroyed. The only troops immediately available for the enterprise were those of the weak 5th Cavalry Division, and it was reported that a mixed force of some twenty thousand Germans and Turks was in the vicinity of Aleppo.

Here lay a golden opportunity for a spectacular victory. If Aleppo could be captured quickly the entire Palestine campaign would be ended at one stroke and not even the fugitive remnants of the Turkish armies would be able to escape. But the risk was great for although, from information received, there seemed to be small likelihood of encountering serious opposition until within striking distance of Aleppo, what would be the position then?

To attempt to take the city by assault with the ridiculously small force available was manifestly out of the question. The only hope of success lay in being able, by bluff, to persuade the enemy to surrender.

On the other hand, it was known that a large Arab force, under Lawrence, was away to the eastward and moving in a north-westerly direction towards Aleppo, so that in the event of the attempt not proving successful and the 5th Division being obliged to fall back, its retreat would be covered and no risk of grave disaster incurred.

After mature consideration General Macandrew, the G.O.C. 5th Division, decided to make the attempt, but realized that it would have to be entirely on his own responsibility and that he, personally, would be held answerable for the consequences in the event of things going wrong.

Very early on the morning of the 21st October the 5th Division marched from Homs, reaching El Rastan about noon on the same day and Zor Defai, just north of Hama, on the afternoon of the 22nd. Ma'arit-el-Naaman was occupied on the 24th and on the morning of the 25th the leading troop of the Division entered Seraikin, only a few miles short of Aleppo. Here some bodies of Turkish cavalry were met with and driven back, but as the advance proceeded serious opposition was encountered from a strong Turkish force in an entrenched position extending from El Ansari to Sheikh Said, and the advance was stopped to enable reconnaissances to be carried out. It was ascertained that the position was held by infantry, estimated to be between 2,000 and 3,000 strong, and that there were between 6,000 and 7,000 more enemy troops in Aleppo. At this juncture, *i.e.*, on the 25th October, a large Arab force, till lately with Lawrence, appeared from the east and occupied Tel Hasil, and consequently General Macandrew decided to attack the city of Aleppo on the following day. During the night, however, the Arabs succeeded in forcing an entry into the town and the Turkish garrison fled, so that the Division marched in on the 26th without opposition. The 14th Brigade was directed to advance along the Alexandretta road and attack any enemy troops who were retreating from Aleppo. A Turkish force of some 3,000 infantry and 400 cavalry with ten guns was encountered, but after putting up a half-hearted resistance, they dispersed during the night and the Brigade halted and put out a line of outposts near El Haritan. On the 28th October Muslimie railway junction was captured by the Arabs and this was taken over by the regiment on the 30th. The Turkish Government now sued for an armistice, which came into effect at noon on the 31st October, thus ending the War.

Upon the conclusion of hostilities, and pending the decisions of the Peace Conference with regard to Syria and Palestine, an army of occupation was required in order to undertake the administration of the country and restore it to a state of law and order.

The area allotted to the Desert Mounted Corps extended from Damascus in the south to some one hundred miles north of Aleppo, and from the Mediterranean coastline to a distance of roughly one hundred miles east of the Euphrates, a total of some 30,000 to 40,000 square miles.

The 14th Brigade was retained in the vicinity of Aleppo, the regiment being stationed at Muslimie Junction.

On the 11th November the following immediate awards were published in Divisional Orders :—

> Bar to Military Cross : Captain F. B. N. Tinley, M.C.
> Indian Order of Merit, 2nd Class : Kote-Duffadar Ahmed Beg.
> Indian Distinguished Service Medal : Rissaldar Bachant Singh, Kote-Duffadar Ragbir Singh, Duffadar Abdul Karim Khan, Acting Lance-Duffadar Subhan Khan, Acting Lance-Duffadar Sundar Singh, Sowar Chanan Singh.

On the 15th November the regiment was inspected by the Corps Commander, Lieutenant-General Sir H. Chauvel, K.C.B., and on the 11th December it took part in lining the streets of Aleppo on the occasion of the triumphal entry of the

Commander-in-Chief, General Sir E. Allenby; otherwise the year ended without incident.

In his comments upon the work of the 5th Division, the Commander-in-Chief remarked: "A brilliant feat of arms. The record of casualties to horses shows the 5th Division to be as good horsemasters as fighters." And in his final despatch he stated that "The gallantry and determination of all ranks and of all arms has been most marked. . . . The Desert Mounted Corps took some 46,000 prisoners during the operations. The complete destruction of the VII and VIII Turkish armies depended mainly on the rapidity with which their communications were reached and on quick decisions in dealing with the enemy's columns as they attempted to escape. The vigorous handling of the cavalry by its leaders and the rapidity of its movements overcame all attempts to delay its progress. The enemy columns, after they had outdistanced the pursuing infantry, were given no time to reorganize or fight their way through."

Since the commencement of the operations, the regiment had marched 571 miles in twenty-seven marching days, with a total of thirteen days' rest, and during this period the 5th Division had fought six actions and taken over 11,000 prisoners and 58 guns.

When the regiment left Sarona on the 17th September, the strength was 461 sabres, with 464 riding horses, and on arrival at Aleppo on the 26th October it was 403 sabres with 323 riding horses, showing a wastage of 58 men and 141 horses.

With regard to the wastage in horses, the greater part was caused by exhaustion or laminitis, due to the absolute necessity of moving fast for days together over rough, stony ground—speed being the all-important factor in ensuring the success of the operations. It was impossible to send sick horses back to the base and so those that were unable to proceed further had to be destroyed. Another cause of wastage was that batteries drew upon the cavalry to make good casualties in the gun teams.

When it is recalled that, owing to the shortage of shipping, no remounts could be sent to Palestine after the middle of 1917 and that all casualties had had to be replaced by horses which had previously been sent (sick or wounded) to remount hospitals, it is a high tribute to the standard of horsemastership in the regiment that the casualties were so few.

With regard to the discrepancy in the figures mentioned above between the number of men and riding horses, which reached Aleppo, it may be of interest to explain that the eighty additional non-commissioned officers and men for whom no horses were available, managed to keep up with the column by capturing camels, ponies and donkeys in the villages through which they passed.

Owing to the necessity of reducing transport to a minimum there was an inadequate supply of both horseshoes and nails (and also of veterinary stores) and the fact that the regiment was able to carry out the long march with so few casualties reflects great credit on the skill and resource of the regimental farriers.

"The experience of the campaign proved that horses cannot be in too 'big' condition at the commencement of operations, provided that they are kept adequately exercised while being conditioned. The really fat, round horses finished both series of operations in better condition than those which had looked harder and more muscular, but not so fat, at the beginning. This was especially the case in the first series, during which the shortage of water was so acute.

* * * * *

"When marching in waterless country the writer used to have a large biscuit tin full of water . . . carried on the dashboard of every gun and wagon.

"At each hourly halt the horses' mouths, nostrils and eyes used to be wiped with a wet—not merely damp—cloth, and this always seemed to refresh them greatly, and to relieve the symptoms of distress due to thirst. A little water was also mixed with the feeds and when the grain was crushed, or there was any bran available, it was found that horses which were off their feed owing to exhaustion would often eat well if fed by hand with small balls made of grain slightly moistened with water."*

The standard forage ration allowed was $9\frac{1}{2}$ lb. of barley (bought locally) and, when grazing was not available, the fodder ration consisted of 10 lb. of chopped barley straw.

On arrival at Aleppo the horses were undoubtedly pulled down and very tired, but after a few weeks' rest they made a remarkable recovery. In this connection the following extract from the *Official History* is quoted:—

"The excellence of the horsemastership throughout the Corps is proved by the comparatively small wastage, when it is recalled that the mount of the average Australian-Yeoman, with kit, arms and ration carried not far short of twenty stone and that the Indians, with a lance added, probably not more than a stone less."

In conclusion, it may be mentioned that the proportion of casualties amongst the pack horses was much higher than among riding horses, which is what one would expect, the pack horse having to carry a dead weight.

---

* *Desert Mounted Corps*, pp. 313-316.

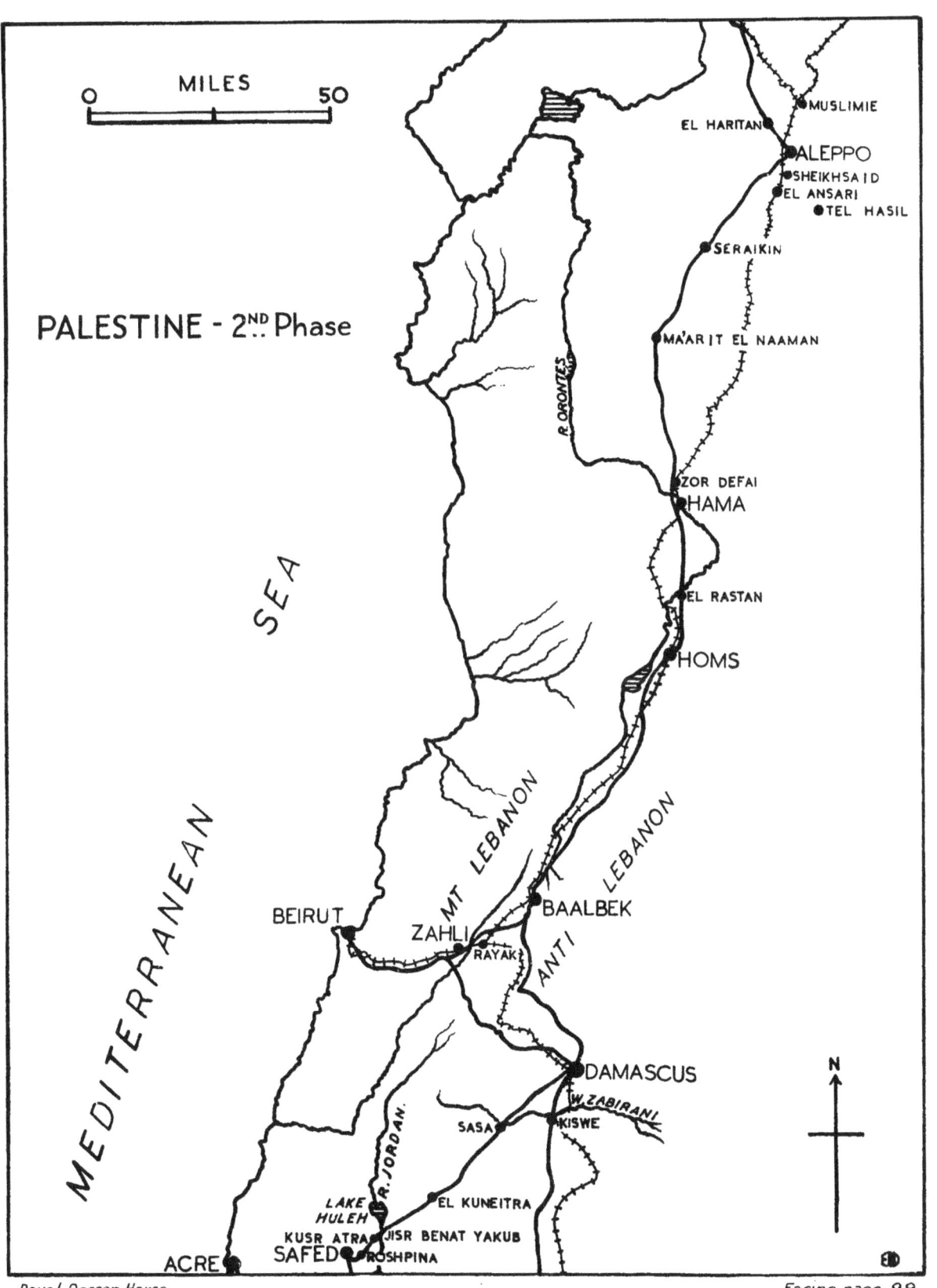

CHAPTER XI

1919 TO 1921

Rioting in Aleppo—Break up of Desert Mounted Corps—Formation of North Force—Beirut—Embarkation for Egypt—Kantara—Farewell Message from Lord Allenby—Return to India—Award to Regiment of Title " Royal "—Grant of Battle Honours—Amalgamation with 29th Lancers (Deccan Horse).

ALTHOUGH the War was over, fifteen months were to elapse before the regiment set foot once more on Indian soil, and therefore it will be of interest to record the principal events which happened during that period.

On the 5th January the following notification was published in Orders :—

" G.R.O. 4771. The Commander-in-Chief desires to place on record his appreciation of the gallant conduct of the undermentioned N.C.Os. and men who courageously volunteered to return to the sinking ship s.s. *Pancras* after she had been torpedoed on 3rd May 1918. The ultimate saving of the vessel was entirely due to their devotion and their untiring efforts at the pumps :—

* * * * *

" No. 1763 Sowar Harpal Singh
     1659   „   Lehri Singh
     1246   „   Nihal Singh
     3515   „   Kapoor Singh } XXth Deccan Horse

* * * * *

" The C.-in-C. directs that an entry be made in their conduct sheets accordingly."

On the 10th February the regiment was moved from Muslimie Junction to the former Turkish barracks, just outside the city of Aleppo. The inhabitants of Aleppo had settled down peacefully and were delighted to be freed from Turkish rule, but in the outlying districts there were many Turkish ex-soldiers, now ragged and in destitution, to whom the sight of the hated Armenians—living in comparative ease and affluence —was a constant source of irritation. Things came to a head on the morning of the 28th February and the regiment received an urgent order to proceed immediately into the city where, it was reported, Turkish ex-soldiers and Arabs were murdering Armenians and looting their houses. Upon reaching the centre of the town patrols, each of the strength of a troop, were despatched in various directions, but it was only in one quarter —on the outskirts of the bazaar—that anything serious was taking place. A reinforcement of forty men under Lieutenant White was despatched to help to restore order and before long the situation was well in hand. The regiment was enabled to return to quarters early in the afternoon, but left " B " Squadron in the town that night as a precautionary measure. There were one or two minor disturbances in the city during March and detachments from the regiment were sent to restore order, but nothing of a serious nature occurred.

On the 6th April the regiment was shocked to learn that Major Cecil Jarvis, M.C., had been killed by a riotous mob in Egypt. The notification in Regimental Orders was as follows :—

" It is with the deepest regret that the Commanding Officer has to announce to the regiment that the O/C Indian Cavalry Base Depot reports the death of Major C. Jarvis, M.C. He appears to have been foully done to death during the recent Egyptian rising. The C.O. would remind all ranks of the sterling example Major Jarvis has always shown in face of the enemy. It was one of gallant and fearless leading with invariably successful results.

"The loss to the regiment of this very gallant officer can only be replaced if Officers and men make the greatest efforts to be always ready, as he was, to face an enemy with determination, and emulate his example."

Major Jarvis was gazetted to the regiment on the 3rd May 1904 and was immensely popular with all ranks. By his gallantry and brilliant leadership he had proved himself to be a first-class cavalry officer. He was severely wounded at Givenchy in 1914.

At Delville Wood in 1916 he commanded the advanced guard, for his leadership of which he received the personal commendation of the Divisional Commander and was awarded the Military Cross.

During the Palestine Campaign his handling of his squadron was always excellent and on the 18th July—some three months after his death—his name appeared in the *London Gazette* as having been awarded the Distinguished Service Order.

On the 16th June Captain E. P. Larkin, who had been taken prisoner at Ghoraniye eleven months previously, rejoined the regiment.

At about this period the Desert Mounted Corps was broken up (the Australian and New Zealand Divisions having left for Egypt) and a new corps was created entitled North Force, under the command of General Barrow, consisting of the 4th and 5th Cavalry Divisions and two infantry divisions.

On the 28th June the following Indian Officers and other ranks reported their departure to attend the Peace Celebrations in London: Rissaldar Konsal Singh, Duffadar Sheo Rup, Sowar Sham Singh.

During the course of the year, with a view to relieving the

monotony, every opportunity was taken to get up football matches, polo tournaments, race meetings and assaults-at-arms, in all of which the regiment took part.

In the assaults-at-arms, a troop of "D" Squadron was twice awarded the first prize for the best-turned-out troop (men and horses) in the whole of the Corps.

On the 26th September the regiment marched from Aleppo to Killis, where it remained until the 7th November and then returned to Aleppo.

Shortly after this the whole of the administration of Northern Syria was handed over to the French, and on the 11th November the regiment bade farewell to Aleppo and marched by easy stages to Beirut, which was reached on the 14th December, and on the 23rd embarked on the transport *Huanchaco* for Kantara Camp.

On the 20th January 1920 intimation was received that the Field-Marshal Commanding-in-Chief had awarded the Indian Distinguished Service Medal to the undermentioned men for gallantry in an action against bandits whilst on detached duty at Afrin Khan on the 14th November 1919: No. 1074 Sowar (A.L.D.) Rajey Ram and No. 1847 Sowar Chandgi Ram, both of "B" Squadron.

On the 20th February 1920 the regiment railed from Kantara to Suez, and on the 23rd March embarked on the transport *Kandy* for India.

On the eve of the regiment's departure the Officer Commanding received the following letter from the Field-Marshal Commanding-in-Chief :—

"On your departure from Egypt and the Egyptian Expeditionary Force, please express to all ranks my high appreciation of the services they have rendered, and their admirable spirit and conduct in all circumstances.

THE ROYAL DECCAN HORSE

"Your regiment has worthily upheld the best fighting traditions of the Indian Cavalry.

"I thank you and wish you a safe return to India.

"(Sgd.) ALLENBY, *Field Marshal*,
"*Commanding-in-Chief.*"

The regiment disembarked at Bombay on the 10th April 1920 (just over five and a half years after it left in 1914), and entrained for Neemuch, rejoining the Depot there on the 17th April.

On the 10th November 1920 the regiment proceeded to Delhi, where it provided the escort for His Excellency the Viceroy upon the occasion of the visit to India of H.R.H. the Duke of Connaught.

In 1921, in recognition of the distinguished services and gallantry of the Indian Army during the Great War, His Majesty was graciously pleased to confer the title "Royal" upon the regiment, the only Indian Cavalry regiment to be so honoured, and in 1926 His Majesty the King-Emperor was graciously pleased to approve of the grant to the regiment of the following Battle Honours in recognition of its services in campaigns during the Great War, 1914–1918 : "Givenchy, 1914," "Somme, 1916," "Bazentin," "Delville Wood," "Flers-Courcelette," "Cambrai, 1917," "France and Flanders, 1914–18," "Megiddo," "Sharon," "Damascus," "Palestine, 1918."

On the 16th July 1921 the XXth Royal Deccan Horse and the 29th Lancers (Deccan Horse) were amalgamated and became henceforth known as

"The Royal Deccan Horse."

APPENDIX A

LIST OF AWARDS RECEIVED

Companion of St. Michael and St. George:
Lieutenant-Colonel G. E. D. Elsmie.

Officer of the British Empire:
Major A. E. H. Ley.

Distinguished Service Order:
Colonel F. Adams.
Major C. Jarvis.
Captain A. C. Ross.
Brevet Major R. B. Worgan.

Military Cross:
Lieutenant A. S. Godfree.
Major C. Jarvis.
Lieutenant F. B. N. Tinley.

Bar to Military Cross:
Captain F. B. N. Tinley.

Legion of Honour (Croix d'Officier):
Lieutenant-Colonel G. E. D. Elsmie.

Officier de l'Ordre de Leopold:
Colonel F. Adams.
Brevet Major R. B. Worgan.

Mérite Agricole:
Colonel F. Adams.

Order of the Nile:
Captain F. C. Guthrie.

Order of British India:
Rissaldar-Major Hanuman Singh.   Rissaldar-Major Nigahya Ram.
       ,,   ,, Konsal Singh.   ,,   ,, Prem Singh.

Indian Order of Merit:
Jemadar Mirza Ahmed Ali Beg.
Duffadar Sardara Singh.
     ,,   Shankar Rao.

Indian Distinguished Service Medal:

Rissaldar Konsal Singh.
   ,,   Sheikh Fayazuddin.
   ,,   Bachant Singh.
   ,,   Dalip Singh.
Jemadar Dalip Singh.
   ,,   Raghbir Singh.
Kote-Duffadar Lehri Singh.
       ,,   Hira Singh.
Duffadar Kasim Khan.
   ,,   Mohd. Zaman Khan.
   ,,   Mirza Mohd. Ali Beg.
   ,,   Rai Singh.
   ,,   Ram Sarup.
   ,,   Abdul Karim Khan.
Salutri Syed Ghulam Mahboob.
Farrier-Major Tika Ram.
Lance-Duffadar Sundar Singh.
        ,,   Shaikh Ahmed Hussain.
        ,,   Mir Raunak Ali.
        ,,   Subhan Khan.
        ,,   Raje Ram.
Ward Orderly Ali Mohd. Khan.
        ,,   Sardara Singh.
Sowar Gokal Singh.
   ,,   Mam Chan.
   ,,   Syed Abdul Majid.
   ,,   Chandgi Ram.
   ,,   Atma Singh.

Meritorious Service Medal:

Kote-Duffadar Teja Singh.
       ,,   Mohd. Ghous.
       ,,   Bharat Singh.
       ,,   Mirza Ahmed Beg.
Quartermaster Duffadar Raghbir Singh.
Farrier-Major Tulja Ram.
Trumpet-Major Sher Mohd. Khan.
Duffadar Dawood Khan.
   ,,   Ghulam Rasul Khan.
   ,,   Amir Khan.
   ,,   Jug Lal.
   ,,   Mohd. Ali.
   ,,   Chair Singh.
   ,,   Ram Nath.
   ,,   Mirza Wilayat Ali Beg.
   ,,   Sheikh Naiz Mohd.
   ,,   Girdhari␃Lal.
   ,,   Mir Akbar Ali.
   ,,   Mool Singh.
   ,,   Abdul Ghani Khan.
   ,,   Abdul Razak Khan.
   ,,   Mahabali Singh.
Duffadar Sheikh Mohd. Ibrahim.
   ,,   Sidi Noor Mohd.
   ,,   Jhanda Singh.
   ,,   Mahabut Singh.
   ,,   Bhim Singh.
Lance-Duffadar Sardar Singh.
        ,,   Sada Singh.
        ,,   Aijaz Ali Khan.
        ,,   Gopal Singh.
        ,,   Raje Ram.
        ,,   Santa Singh.
        ,,   Chandgi Ram III.
        ,,   Lehri Singh.
        ,,   Ahmed Khan.
        ,,   Tamizuddin Khan.
Farrier Phuman Singh.
   ,,   Dila Ram.
Trumpeter Sheikh Zahoor Mohd.
Ward Orderly Damodar Rao.
Sowar Raghbir Singh.
   ,,   Sawai Singh.

Croix de Guerre (France):

Kote-Duffadar Sardara Singh.
Duffadar Shankar Rao.
Lance-Duffadar Syed Abdul Majid.

Médaille Militaire (France):

Quartermaster-Duffadar Bhawani Singh.

Mentioned in Despatches :

Colonel F. Adams.
Lieutenant-Colonel G. E. D. Elsmie.
Lieutenant F. G. Guthrie.
Major C. Jarvis.
Major A. C. Ross.
Lieutenant F. B. N. Tinley.
Captain R. B. Worgan.

Rissaldar-Major Prem Singh.
Jemadar Sher Singh.
Duffadar Amir Khan.
    ,,   Ghulam Rasul.
Sowar Harphul Singh.
  ,, Lehri.
  ,, Nihal.

APPENDIX B

British Officers who served with the Regiment in the Field during the Great War

Abbay, Captain.
Adams, Colonel F.
Addington, Lieutenant Honble. R. A.
Barrow, Second-Lieutenant W. W.
Burmester, Captain.
Burt, Captain.
Chamberlayne, Major A.
Clark, Captain W. H.
Clarke, Major C. F.
Cobb, Lieutenant W.
Cocker, Lieutenant W. R.
Collins, Captain J. R.
Coventry, Lieutenant.
Craster, Major W. S.
Day, Lieutenant E. R.
Dening, Major L. E.
Drake-Brockman, Lieutenant.
Dyke, Major O. M.
Elsmie, Lieutenant-Colonel G. E. D.
Figg, Lieutenant W. G.
Foa, Lieutenant A. H.
Gererd, Lieutenant H. J. F.
Glasspoole, Captain L. A.
Godfree, Captain A. S.
Gregson, Major C. D.
Gretton, Captain.
Guthrie, Captain F. C.
Hallifax, Captain H. F.
Hallifax, Second-Lieutenant J.
Hamley, Lieutenant W. S. C.
Heaton-Armstrong, Captain J. D.
Henderson, Major R. W.
Hopkins, Captain W. J.
Humfrey, Lieutenant H. B.
James, Captain F.
Jarvis, Major C.
Larkin, Captain E. P.

Lawford, Lieutenant E. E.
MacAdam, Lieutenant H. C. V. G.
McEuen, Captain J. S.
Mackenzie, Captain C. A. C.
Maxwell, Lieutenant J. F.
Meyar, Second-Lieutenant W. R. M.
Mulloy, Captain N. F. C.
Murray, Lieutenant V.
Percy-Smith, Major V.
Pike, Captain W. H.
Pollitt, Lieutenant H. T.
Rayneau, Lieutenant L. A.
Robertson, Captain E. P. S.
Robinson, Second-Lieutenant F. R. H.
Ross, Brevet Lieutenant-Colonel A. C.
Rust, Lieutenant F. H.
Ryan, Lieutenant C. C. L.
Salvesen, Captain E. T.
Schofield, Lieutenant A. J.
Schokman, Lieutenant C. C.
Simpson, Lieutenant J. N.
Smith, Lieutenant D. R.
Souter, Major A.
Swayne, Lieutenant R. P. N.
Sykes, Second-Lieutenant W. D.
Tennant, Lieutenant-Colonel E.
Tinley, Major F. B. N.
Turner, Lieutenant-Colonel F. W. C.
Tyrrell, Major A. C. L.
Wallace, Lieutenant A. M.
White, Lieutenant C. W. G.
Wilson, Lieutenant J. F. S.
Wilson, Captain T. K.
Woodman, Lieutenant J. B.
Worgan, Brevet Lieutenant-Colonel R. B.

Medical Officers :

Berryman, Captain R. C. P., I.M.S.
Calvert, Captain W., I.M.S.
Campbell, Lieutenant D., R.A.M.C.
Firth, Captain I. G. M., R.A.M.C.

Fleming, Lieutenant-Colonel, I.M.S.
Griffith, Captain D. W., R.A.M.C.
Menon, Lieutenant C. V. A., I.M.S.
Plumley, Captain A. G. G., R.A.M.C.

(The rank shown is the highest which was held whilst actually serving with the regiment in the War.)

APPENDIX C

Roll of Officers and Men who lost their Lives in the Great War

Lieutenant-Colonel G. E. D. Elsmie, C.M.G. (with 25th Cavalry).
Major   C. Jarvis, D.S.O., M.C.
"   C. F. Clarke.
"   V. Percy-Smith.
Captain   J. S. McEuen.
"   C. A. C. Mackenzie.
Lieutenant   A. Lawford.
"   J. F. S. Wilson.

Interpreter M. Azemar (French Army).
Rissaldar-Major Jharmal Singh.
"   Amir Mohd. Khan.
"   Nighaya Ram.
Rissaldar Mir Hadayat Ali.
"   Mahbub Khan I.
"   Mahbub Khan II.
"   Ganga Bishan.
"   Dalip Singh.
Jemadar Dalip Singh.
"   Samund Singh.
Kote-Duffadar Sagir Mohd. Khan.
Duffadar Mirza Munawar Ali Beg.
"   Prag Singh.
"   Mansab Ali Khan.
"   Sajjan Singh.
"   Mewa Singh.
"   Jehangir Khan.
"   Bukkan Singh.
"   Karam Sher Khan.
"   Dall Singh.
"   Ram Saroop.
"   Jai Lall.
"   Bal Ram.
"   Ahmed Hussain Khan.
Lance-Duffadar Mustafa Khan.
"   Sheikh Mohd. Akbar.
"   Nand Singh.
"   Sardar Singh.
"   Sher Singh.
"   Munshi Singh.
Lance-Duffadar Didar Singh.
"   Amir Singh.
"   Jage Ram.
"   Ali Mohd. Khan.
"   Bhartoo Singh.
"   Ratti Ram.
"   Daya Ram.
"   Arjan Singh.
"   Govind Singh.
"   Ram Saroop.
"   Abdulla Beg.
"   Chajjan Singh.
"   Nadir Singh.
"   Kishan Singh.
"   Partap Singh.
"   Sham Singh.
"   Afzal Shah Khan.
"   Pirthi Singh.
Sowar Zorawar Khan.
"   Arjan Singh.
"   Lall Singh.
"   Bir Singh.
"   Mansa Singh.
"   Waryam Singh.
"   Chur Singh.
"   Dira Singh.
"   Saugor Singh.
"   Harnam Singh.
"   Mustafa Khan.
"   Noor Khan.
"   Sheikh Shabuddin.

Sowar Naseeb Khan.
" Azizuddin Khan.
" Inayat Khan.
" Ratton Singh.
" Sawan Singh.
" Siri Chand.
" Jug Lall.
" Gokal Singh.
" Kishan Lall.
" Sukh Lall.
" Roop Chand.
" Hira Singh.
" Sada Ram.
" Badloo Ram.
" Ramji Lall.
" Abbas Ali Khan.
" Jammon Singh.
" Harphool Singh.
" Ganda Singh.
" Jauddin Khan.
" Mir Fiyaz Ali.
" Mansab Khan.
" Chanda Singh.
" Siddi Ali Kumer.
" Yaseen Khan.
" Mohd. Hanif.
" Ram Sarup.
" Nand Singh.
" Dharam Singh.
" Neki Ram.
" Ali Sher Khan.
" Chunni Singh.
" Sheikh Mohd. Ali.
" Nand Ram.
" Mohd. Zahoor.
" Jagath Singh.
" Hasnuddin Khan.
" Sudhan Singh.
" Chandgi Ram.
" Chandan Singh.
" Soorja.
" Kude Ram.
" Khushi Ram.
" Sath Narayan Singh.

Sowar Chotoo Singh.
" Raghunath Rao.
" Dani Ram.
" Mir Imdad Ali.
" Santa Singh.
" Sher Singh.
" Harnam Singh.
" Sheikh Baba.
" Neki Ram.
" Attar Singh.
" Akbar Khan.
" Inder Singh.
" Dongar Singh.
" Harnam Singh.
" Abhey Ram.
" Sohan Pal.
" Kala Singh.
" Kanhiya Singh.
" Fakira Singh.
" Niader Singh.
" Lall Singh.
" Udey Ram.
" Ram Sarup.
" Gokal Singh.
" Ganga Ram.
" Kewal Singh.
" Mahboob Khan.
" Hyder Khan.
" Abdul Kader.
" Gurbha Singh.
" Bhajan Singh.
" Sheikh Moinudin.
" Jhanno Singh.
" Sri Chand.
" Ahmed Hussain.
Farrier Cheloo.
Mochi Erannah.
Bhisty Mohd. Yakoob.
Ward Orderly Kundan Singh.
" Naranjan Singh.
Sweeper Khewan Singh.
" Kupru.
Private Servant Ambrose.
" Bal Kishan.

APPENDIX D

The Silladar System

ALTHOUGH all Indian Silladar cavalry regiments were raised and maintained in accordance with one general plan, it is unlikely that the interior-economy arrangements of any two regiments were identical, and therefore the details given in the following description are those which were customary in the cavalry regiments of the late Hyderabad Contingent.

Before proceeding to describe the origin and evolution of the Silladar System it will be necessary to explain the meanings of a few technical terms.

A *Silladar* was the *owner* of an *Assami*.

An *Assami* was the "Property," comprising the horse, saddlery, equipment, transport, arms, etc.; in fact, everything required by the soldier with the exception of his uniform.

A *Paigah*.—In the early days any number of *Assamis* could be owned by one person (not necessarily a soldier) and two or more *Assamis* constituted what was known as a *Paigah*.

A *Barghir*.—A trooper who did not own an *Assami*, but was mounted on a *Silladar's* horse, was called a *Barghir*. The *Barghir* received a dismounted soldier's pay, the balance of the contract pay going to the *Silladar* for the upkeep of the *Assami*.

In the days of the Honourable East India Company, when large numbers of mounted troops were required at short notice in order to deal with some sudden emergency, the usual method adopted was to approach some friendly chieftain with a view to hiring his levies, for a specified period, in return for an agreed monthly payment per head for each mounted soldier furnished. By the terms of the agreement the chieftain (and not the East India Company) undertook the responsibility of clothing, equipping and feeding his men and horses and for providing any transport required, but the Company had the right to insist that the horses were maintained in good, serviceable condition and that the equipment supplied was sufficient for the purpose. The Silladar, however, was at liberty to feed his horse (or horses) on whatever he liked, and this right was never relinquished, even when the irregular levies were converted into regular cavalry and incorporated in the Indian Army. Even up to the time of the Great War there was no such thing as a "standard ration" for the horses of Silladar regiments. The Squadron Commander might, and probably would, suggest what he considered to be a suitable ration of forage and fodder for the season of the year, but every Silladar was at liberty to vary the ration as he pleased. The one and only condition was, that the horse must always come up to the standard required by the Squadron Commander. As the Silladar had to pay for his horse's food out of his own pocket it was obviously to his advantage to study his animal and find out the most economical way of feeding it.

The remedy for bad horsemastership was very simple. The Squadron Commander took the horse into his own stable, got it into proper condition and the Silladar paid the food bill! It was very rarely that this step had to be taken—a word of warning was usually sufficient.

It would be difficult to suggest a better method of teaching men the art of horsemastership, and this is borne out by the fact that, year after year, the Inspection Reports of the regiments of the Hyderabad Contingent Cavalry invariably commended the condition of the horses.

In the very early days, as has been explained, any person, whether belonging to the regiment or not, could be a Silladar and own a Paigah (*i.e.*, any number of Assamis). As this proved to be a profitable investment it was not long before a considerable number of the Assamis got into the hands of sowcars,* banniahs† and such-like people, and this proved to be very detrimental to the discipline of the regiments. In 1860 the newly established Government of India issued orders that, in future, only persons enlisted in a regiment could be Silladars and own Assamis.

In 1875 this proviso was further restricted by making it compulsory for each man (with a few minor exceptions) enlisted in a cavalry regiment to become a " Khudaspah " or one-horse Silladar. In other words, each trooper had to own the horse he rode and provide everything included in the Assami.

Prior to this period it had been the custom for men enlisting in a regiment to bring their own horses and equipment with them, and in order to maintain some hold over them and prevent desertions, it was obligatory for each recruit, upon enlistment, to place a deposit, equivalent to one and a half month's pay, in the " Amanath Fund."‡ On the completion of his term of service this sum was refunded to him, but it would be forfeited in the event of desertion.

By the new regulations, however, the recruit was now no longer permitted to bring his own horse and equipment, but, instead, was obliged to pay to the regiment, upon enlistment, the full cash value of the Assami, in return for which the regiment undertook to provide him with horse, saddlery, stable gear, arms, equipment, uniform, quarters, stabling and transport, but for the maintenance of which, in good serviceable condition, he remained responsible.

When a Silladar left the regiment he was repaid the whole of the *Assami price*, the regiment retaining the Assami, which was then transferred to the incoming recruit. (It will thus be seen that what a recruit paid for his Assami when he enlisted in a Silladar regiment was merely a " deposit " which was returned to him in full when he left.)

The estimated value of an Assami varied in different regiments, but in the Hyderabad Contingent Cavalry it was fixed at Rs650.

As has been stated, the Silladar was responsible for the proper maintenance of every item included in his Assami, and in order to provide for the cost of repairs and replacements, monthly deductions were made from his pay and credited to the appropriate regimental funds. For example, let us assume the net cost of a five-year-old troop horse to be Rs360. Excluding accident or disease, this horse should do ten years' service before being " cast " for age—and therefore its replacement value had to be recovered from the Silladar during that period. This meant that Rs36 per annum (or Rs3 per mensem) had to be deducted from his pay and credited to the Horse Fund. The same principle was followed for the replacement of saddlery, equipment, tents, barracks, stables, transport animals, etc. In this way very large sums of money were held in trust by the regimental authorities—every penny of which belonged to the men. This money, however, was not allowed to remain idle but was invested in Government securities, the interest accruing being credited to a Regimental

* Sowcar, moneylender.
† Banniah, petty trader and shopkeeper.
‡ For some now forgotten reason the " Amanath " deposit system was retained right up to the end, although its *raison d'être* no longer existed.

(or general purposes) Fund. Another source of income to the Regimental Fund arose from the sale of Assamis to the incoming recruit. Few, if any, were in a position to pay down in cash the whole of the Assami price so that the balance was advanced to them from the Regimental Fund and interest charged at the rate of $6\frac{1}{4}$ per cent. per annum.

The Regimental Fund constituted a most useful and necessary " reserve " from which sums could be drawn to meet unforeseen or exceptional expenses, without putting any financial strain upon the Silladars. By way of example a few typical cases may be given :—

(1) In the event of the regiment being required to furnish a detachment for ceremonial parades at a Coronation or a Durbar, the men composing it would be supplied with new uniforms at the expense of the Regimental Fund.

(2) The cost of sending regimental teams to compete at assaults-at-arms, polo, hockey or football matches was wholly or in part paid by the fund.

(3) It was customary to invite all pensioned Indian Officers and men to come to the annual regimental sports and thus to make it an occasion for a regimental reunion, the fund paying the railway fares of all those who attended.

There were scores of other cases where the assistance of the Regimental Fund was called for, but the three mentioned above will suffice to show the useful purpose it served.

I think it will be agreed by all who have had practical experience of the Silladar System that one great drawback to it was the enormous amount of book-keeping that it entailed.

Every month a Squadron Commander had to see that the correct deductions had been made from each man's pay and credited to the different funds, such as : Amanath Fund, Horse Fund, Saddlery Fund, Tent Fund, Barrack Fund (commonly called " Line Fund "), Forge Fund, Regimental Fund, and several more.

In addition to this the Second-in-Command (who was also the Accounts Officer) had to spend hours every day checking entries of deposits and disbursements in the Regimental Day Book and Ledgers.

But this was only part of the extra labour and responsibility laid upon the shoulders of the British Officer. For some unknown reason, the Government of India refused to allow Silladar regiments to purchase any of their requirements from either the Army Ordnance or Supply Departments; consequently everything had to be bought in the open market (at correspondingly higher prices—value for value). For example, if new saddles were required, samples and estimates had to be obtained from various saddlers—generally from England—and then a committee of British and Indian Officers would meet and decide as to which firm the order should be given to. The same procedure was followed in the case of every other article that had to be purchased, including material for uniforms, greatcoats, tents and the iron for horseshoes, etc. As none of the members of these committees were trade experts the risk of making an unsatisfactory purchase was very great and if this did sometimes happen it entailed a heavy loss to the unfortunate Silladar.

Up to twenty years before the Great War service in a Silladar cavalry regiment was so popular that it was customary for there to be a score of applicants for any vacancy in the strength. This was probably due to the fact that a Silladar could and did save a considerable amount each month out of his Assami pay of Rs20 a month. But each year higher and ever higher standards of quality in both horses and equipment were demanded by Army Headquarters without any commensurate increase in the Silladar's pay, so that latterly it was only with the greatest difficulty that he could make ends meet. At the time of the outbreak of the Great War the Silladar's monthly pay amounted to Rs34, out of which Rs9 had to be deducted by the regiment for the upkeep of the items included in the Assami. This left him with a balance of Rs25 to meet the cost of feeding his horse and baggage mule, of keeping up his uniform and necessaries and, in addition, of maintaining himself and his family.

But from his total pay of Rs34, provided by the Government, one should, in equity, deduct the amount of interest due to the Silladar upon the capital sum provided by him for the purchase of his Assami (the several items of which were provided *free* by the State to the non-Silladar). Thus, if we assume the purchase price of the Assami to have been Rs650, the interest thereon (at $6\frac{1}{4}$ per cent. per annum) would, roughly, amount to $Rs3\frac{1}{2}$ a month, so that the actual pay received by the sowar was only $Rs30\frac{1}{2}$ a month—equivalent to about one shilling and sixpence a day in English money. In return for this very moderate expenditure the State obtained a highly trained body of cavalry, maintained permanently on a war footing and ready to march, with all necessary transport, at the shortest notice.

That this latter statement is no idle boast is proved by the following extracts from the official records. As far back as 1832, Major-General Sleigh, C.B., reported as follows:

" The horses, generally, show a good deal of blood . . . they make extraordinary marches, sixty miles in a night and seldom, if ever, leave a man behind; indeed the men would fancy themselves disgraced if unable to proceed with their comrades. . . . The great advantage these corps possess over the Regular cavalry is *they move without delay and never require aid or assistance from the commissariat. They have everything within themselves that the most efficient commissariat could give a King's regiment and could, on emergency, get twenty-four hours' start of any of them.*"

Then again, in the year 1879 the 3rd Cavalry, Hyderabad Contingent, was stationed at Mominabad, a small cantonment, eighty-two miles from the nearest railway station, to which there was only a cart-track over "black cotton" fields and these, at the time of the following incident, were in a boggy condition from rain. Without previous warning the regiment received orders to proceed at once to Karachi to take part in the Second Afghan War.

At four o'clock in the morning *just fourteen hours after the receipt of the order, the regiment marched out of cantonments.* By the morning of the fourth day it had entrained 450 men and horses and 300 baggage animals, complete with followers and baggage, and by the sixth day it had embarked in five transports at Bombay.

This readiness to take the field at the shortest notice was occasionally put to the test by General Officers at their inspections. Without any previous warning a named troop or squadron would be ordered to parade in marching order in an hour's time and would then be directed to proceed, at once, on reconnaissance duty to some village situated some fifty or sixty miles away, with orders to return next day, by a stated time, with their report.

Could this be carried out nowadays by regular cavalry?

It will be patent, even from the foregoing very brief description, that the Silladar System was bound to break down on active service unless regiments were enabled to replace their requirements in horses, clothing and equipment from the army supply departments. Realizing this, the Government of India decided, in 1905, that when on active service Silladar regiments would be permitted to do so; but why this regulation was not extended to meet peace-time requirements is not known. After the conclusion of the Great War the Government abolished the Silladar System *in toto* and now all Indian cavalry regiments are maintained on the British pattern.

Although it is not disputed that there were defects in the Silladar System, there were none that could not have been remedied without forfeiting its many advantages, amongst which were the following :—

(1) Ability to take the field at short notice, complete with transport.
(2) Unsurpassed method of teaching horsemastership.
(3) Training in self-reliance, as opposed to being " spoon-fed."
(4) The prestige (*izzat*) the Silladar felt at owning his own horse.
(5) A better and more intelligent class of recruits, owing to the fact that their parents had to be persons of some standing in order to be able to provide the amount required to purchase an Assami.

APPENDIX E

Cavalry in Modern War

ALTHOUGH, in these days, it is the fashion to regard cavalry as out of date and useful only for ceremonial occasions, it may not be out of place to give a few extracts from Lieutenant-Colonel Preston's book, *The Desert Mounted Corps*.

In an introductory letter, Lieutenant-General Sir Harry Chauvel, K.C.B., C.M.G., commanding the Desert Mounted Corps, writes :—

" As a work of Cavalry Tactics, I trust it will be of some value to the student of Military History, and, if it does nothing else, it must demonstrate to the world that the horse-soldier is just as valuable in modern warfare as he ever has been in the past.

" Indeed, the whole of the operations in Palestine and Syria, under General Allenby, were textbook illustrations of the perfect combination of all arms, both in attack and defence, and the last operations in this theatre which led to the total destruction of the Turkish arms and the elimination of Germany's Allies from the War, could not have been undertaken without large masses of Cavalry."

* * * * *

" The long apprenticeship of the Indian Cavalry to the trench warfare of the Western Front had robbed them of none of their dash and brilliancy in the open warfare to which they were so eminently fitted."

On pages 26 and 27 Colonel Preston relates how cavalry were able to cross a flat plain, devoid of cover, for a distance of two miles, against infantry strongly entrenched and supported by several batteries, with comparatively little loss.

31ST OCTOBER 1917.

" The day was now far gone and the advance seemed to be at a standstill. General Chaytor then put in his reserve brigade to co-operate in the attack on Tel el Saba from the South. General Cox, commanding the Brigade, directed the 2nd A.L.H. Regiment on the two block houses and the 3rd on Tel el Saba.

" From the shelter of a small wadi, some three miles south of the hill, the two regimental commanders scrutinized the open plain in front of them in an effort to find some covered way of approach. None could be found, so the two commanders determined to make a dash for it mounted, and get as near as possible before dismounting to continue the attack on foot. Deploying from the wadi, the two regiments swung out into line of troop columns, at wide intervals, and galloped forward over the open plain in full view of the enemy. Several Turkish batteries at once opened fire on them, but they were advancing so fast that the enemy gunners seemed to be unable to get the range, and but little damage was caused by their fire. It was not, indeed, until the regiments came under machine-gun fire that casualties began to occur, and, even then, our loss was slight, probably owing to the steep angle of descent of machine-gun bullets at long ranges and to the difficulty of finding and keeping the range. At 1,500 yards from the position they rode into a convenient depression and here they dismounted and continued the advance on foot.

" . . . . Now that they were on foot, and moving slowly, they began to suffer severely, whereas they had advanced mounted for over two miles with scarcely any casualties."

On page 53 the author describes how ten troops saved the situation by charging the enemy's guns, which were in a prepared position and consisted of one field and one mountain battery (with four machine guns between the batteries) and three heavy howitzers in support. The whole were captured with a loss on our side of only seventy-five men.

8TH NOVEMBER 1917.

"At about 3 p.m., as the right flank of the 60th Division was approaching Huj, it came suddenly under a devastating fire at close range from several concealed batteries of enemy artillery, which, with two battalions of infantry, were covering the withdrawal of the Eighth Army Headquarters.

"The country was rather like Salisbury Plain, rolling downland without any cover, and our troops suffered severely from the murderous fire.

"Major-General Shea, commanding the Division, finding Colonel Gray-Cheape of the Warwick Yeomanry close by him, requested him to charge the enemy guns at once.

"Colonel Cheape collected a few troops of his own regiment that he had with him, and some of the Worcester Yeomanry, and led them away to the right front.

"Taking advantage of a slight rise in the ground to the east of the enemy position, he succeeded in leading his troops to within 800 yards of the Turkish guns, unseen. He then gave the order to charge, and the ten troops galloped over the rise and raced down upon the flank of the enemy guns. The Turks had in position one battery of field, and one of mountain, guns, with four machine guns on a low hill behind the two batteries and three heavy howitzers further behind.

"As our cavalry appeared, thundering over the rise, the Turks sprang to their guns and swung them round, firing point-blank into the charging horsemen. The infantry, leaping on the limbers, blazed away with their rifles till they were cut down. There was no thought of surrender; every man stuck to his gun or rifle to the last. The leading troops of the Cavalry dashed into the first enemy battery. The following troops, swinging to the right, took the three heavy howitzers almost in their stride, leaving the guns silent, the gun crews dead or dying, and galloped round the hill, to fall upon the mountain battery from the rear, and cut the Turkish gunners to pieces in a few minutes.

"The third wave, passing the first battery, where a fierce sabre and bayonet fight was going on between our cavalry and the enemy, raced up the slope at the machine guns. Many saddles were emptied in that few yards, but the charge was irresistible. In a few minutes the enemy guns were silenced, their crews killed and the whole position was in our hands.

"General Kress von Kressenstein and his staff, who were still at Huj when our cavalry made this charge, narrowly escaped capture, and had to leave everything behind them in their hurried flight, even to their wireless code-book."

* * * * *

"This was the first time that our troops had 'got home' properly with the modern cavalry thrusting sword, and an examination of the enemy dead afterwards proved what a fine weapon it is. Our losses were heavy. Of the 170-odd who took part in the charge, seventy-five were killed and wounded, and all within the space of ten minutes."

* * * * *

"The action was of interest as an indication of what may be accomplished, under suitable conditions, by even a very small force of cavalry when resolutely led.

"The charge was made on the spur of the moment, with little preliminary reconnaissance of the ground, without fire support and with the equivalent of little more than two squadrons of cavalry. It resulted in the capture of eleven guns and four machine guns, and the complete destruction of a strong point of enemy resistance, at a cost of seventy-five casualties."

* * * * *

"There was considerable divergence of opinion in the cavalry as to the best method to be employed in a mounted attack . . . subject to the principle that fire support should always be provided if possible, and that the line of fire and the direction of the mounted attack should be as nearly as possible at right angles to one another. . . . The 5th Mounted Brigade had been practising the following method for the attack of lightly entrenched troops. A regiment charged in column of squadrons in line, with a distance of 150 to 200 yards between squadrons. The leading squadron charged with the sword, and, having passed over the enemy position, galloped straight on to attack any enemy supports that might be coming up. The remainder of the regiment charged without swords. The second squadron galloped over the trench while the enemy were still in a state of confusion, dismounted on the farther side, and attacked from the rear with the bayonet.

"The third squadron dismounted before reaching the trench, and went in with the bayonet from the front. Two machine guns accompanied this last squadron and came into action on one or both flanks, as the situation demanded, to deal with any counter-attack that might develop. If more than one regiment took part in the attack, the machine guns, of course, moved on the outer flanks of the regiments. Unfortunately this brigade never had an opportunity of putting this method to the test, but the 4th A.L.H. Brigade used it in a modified form at Beersheba, with excellent results."

* * * * *

"Where a mounted attack had to cover a considerable distance of open ground before reaching charging distance, the most usual formation was in column of squadrons in line of troop columns. Our own gunners were of opinion that this formation offered the most difficult target to artillery, provided the interval between troops was not less than 25 yards and the distance between squadrons not less than 100 yards.

"The experience of the campaign seemed to point to the fact that cavalry also suffered less from machine-gun fire in this formation than in any other, at any rate at ranges beyond 1,000 yards."

On page 209 Colonel Preston relates how a single cavalry regiment—supported by armoured cars—charged a Turkish infantry battalion, reinforced with several machine guns, and either killed or captured the entire force, with the result that our troops were enabled to debouch from the Musmas defile without opposition.

LEJJUN. 20TH SEPTEMBER 1918.

"As soon as it was light enough to see, the troops commenced to move out into the Plain of Esdraelon. They were none too soon. As . . . the advanced guard of the Division debouched from the defile, a Turkish battalion, with several machine guns, was deploying in the plain below.

"The 2nd Lancers were leading, accompanied by the armoured cars. Taking in the situation at a glance, Captain Davison, commanding the regiment, ordered the cars to engage the enemy in front with their machine guns, supported by one squadron of his regiment. Taking the other two squadrons with him, he galloped

THE ROYAL DECCAN HORSE

along a slight depression to the right and charged the Turks on their left flank. The two squadrons went right through the enemy from left to right, killing 46 with the lance. The survivors of the battalion, about 500 in all, were taken prisoners. The Turks fought well, firing steadily till they were ridden down, but the rapid work of the cavalry gave them no chance.

" The whole action did not take more than five minutes, and furnished a perfect little example of sound shock tactics—movement and fire at right angles to one another.

" Had our cavalry been a few hours later, this battalion would have been at the defile at the top of the pass, and might have caused a delay that would have been fatal to the success of the operations."

Another lesson learnt in the Palestine Campaign, was that, for cavalry acting mounted, the lance is immeasurably superior to the sword.

APPENDIX F

Commandants of the Regiment from the Year 1818

Lieutenant John Southerland.
" Eric Southerland.
Captain Charles Macleod.
" John Child Shakespear.
" Thomas William Clagett.
Colonel W. Murray.
Lieutenant-Colonel Hugh Watson.
" C. B. Farrington.
" H. S. Stewart.
" G. Adye.
" F. S. Gwatkin, C.B.
" E. F. H. McSwiney, C.B., D.S.O.
" F. H. Yate.
" A. A. Jones.
" G. E. D. Elsmie, C.M.G.
" E. Tennant.
" F. Adams, D.S.O.
" L. F. Arthur, D.S.O., O.B.E.
" W. J. Lambert, D.S.O.
" R. J. H. Baddeley, M.C.
" G. P. Morris, O.B.E.
" F. Gwatkin, D.S.O., M.C.
" A. G. O. M. Mayne, D.S.O.
" F. B. N. Tinley, M.C.

29th LANCERS (DECCAN HORSE)
1914—1920

FOREWORD

BY

BRIGADIER-GENERAL W. J. LAMBERT, D.S.O.
Last Commandant of the 29th Lancers (Deccan Horse)

THE early history of the 29th Lancers being almost identical with that of the XXth Deccan Horse, it was very fitting that these two regiments, which had so much in common, should have been amalgamated.

In Chapter I of the History of the XXth Deccan Horse a brief sketch is given of this early history, but a few additional points, which have not been touched on, are added here, together with a brief summary of the services of the 29th Lancers prior to 1914.

The regiment was formed from the Nizam's Horse in Berar in 1816, under the title of Nawab Murtaza Yar Jung's (Captains Hallis and Smith) Risala.

In 1826 it became the 2nd Regiment, Nizam's Cavalry, and in 1854 2nd Cavalry, Hyderabad Contingent.

In 1890 it became the 2nd Lancers, Hyderabad Contingent, and in 1903 was transferred to the Bombay Command and incorporated with the Regular Indian Cavalry, with the title 29th Lancers (Deccan Horse).

In 1921, after the return of the XXth Deccan Horse and the 29th Lancers to India from the Great War, these two regiments were amalgamated in Bolarum (the old headquarters of the Hyderabad Contingent), and designated "The Royal Deccan Horse," under the command of Lieutenant-Colonel (now Brigadier-General) W. J. Lambert, D.S.O.

It is interesting to note that the Hyderabad Contingent Cavalry was evolved from the armed levies of the native chieftains of Berar. The necessity for the reform of these trained bands was ascribed to their inefficiency and inability to cope with the predatory Pindaris, whose mobility was such as to enable them to escape from the heavy British cavalry.

In 1854 there were four Hyderabad Contingent Cavalry regiments stationed in the Deccan. Bolarum was the headquarters, the other stations being Aurangabad, Hingoli and Mominabad. Every five years the regiments changed stations in rotation, but never left the Deccan, except on active service.

In 1875 Brigadier-General T. Wright, C.B., was appointed to the command of the Hyderabad Contingent and introduced the Silladar System on the lines of the Bengal Cavalry.

In 1903, on becoming the 29th Lancers, the regiment was transferred to the Bombay Command and left Hyderabad, Deccan, for the first time, going to Sirur, the old Poona Horse station.

Subsequently it moved to other stations in India, but returned to Bolarum in 1920, after the conclusion of the Great War.

The Class Squadron System was adopted in 1895. At that time the regiment was composed of three squadrons: one of Deccan Muhammadans, one of Sikhs, and one of Jats. (On the break-up of the 3rd Lancers, in 1903, another squadron of Jats was added.)

The Deccan Muhammadan of the right type was the perfect article for light cavalry, his horsemastership, skill-at-arms and intelligence being quite above the average, but unfortunately this class has now become almost extinct, and is no longer recruited for the cavalry.

HYDERABAD CONTINGENT CAVALRY
("REFORMED HORSE")
1845

THE ROYAL DECCAN HORSE

The regiment in the early days was mounted on the Deccan horse, a countrybred, perhaps not up to the standard of the regular cavalry, but capable of enduring great fatigue and subsisting on very little grain.

In 1845 the horses were Arabs and Countrybreds of various classes, and between 1880 and 1900 almost entirely Arabs, which were bought in Bombay by British Officers of the regiment. In 1900 the waler from Australia began to replace the Arab, and subsequently the regiment was almost entirely mounted on walers.

The horsemastership of this regiment was second to none, and when it left India for the Great War it was one of the best-mounted Indian cavalry regiments in India. Due testimony was paid to this quality—which was upheld even in Flanders and Palestine.

With regard to armament and equipment :—

In 1816 English carbines were given to one-third of the men, the remainder being armed with pistol, sword, and matchlock.

In 1880 the regiment was armed with lances, and in 1884 Snider carbines and revolvers were issued, followed by the Martini-Henry and, in 1901, by the Lee-Enfield.

Summary of Services

In 1818 the Risala of Nawab Murtaza Yar Jung served, under Lieutenant John Sutherland, in the operations against the rebel Dharmaji, also under Captain Hallis on the Wardha river in Central India.

In 1826 the 2nd Cavalry, under Captain Gordon, was employed in quelling disturbances of Rohillas and Arabs in the direction of Parbanhi and Nander.

In 1828 a squadron of the 2nd Cavalry was employed,

under Captain Adam, in quelling a disturbance at Phalmari, north of Aurangabad.

In 1829 a detachment, under Lieutenant Malony, was engaged in pursuit of freebooters in the Ajanta and Dewalghat districts, and a troop, under Lieutenant Lang, marched against three hundred Bhils near Lonar.

In 1830 a squadron, under Lieutenant Jackson, took part in the reduction of the fort of Kaptak.

In 1831 a squadron of the regiment was engaged in the operations at Wanparti, and in August and September of the same year, twenty-two troopers were employed in the reduction of a refractory zemindar at Raichur.

In 1832, on the 26th March, the 2nd Cavalry, under Captain Inglis, surprised and captured the freebooter Kundi Reddi, after a forced march from Bolarum. In June a squadron, under Captain Tomkyns, made a forced march of eighty miles, in two and a half days, to Golagaon, where a refractory zemindar, Jaloji, was captured. In August and September Captain Inglis was out with the regiment in pursuit of Gurnath Reddi and the Zemindari Asa, the latter being taken prisoner in the fort of Kosam on the 9th September.

From December 1832 to February 1833 a squadron saw service in the neighbourhood of Guntur.

In April 1838 a troop, under Captain Johnston, assisted in quelling a riot at Akola.

In 1842 the regiment was engaged in the Gulbarga district in checking the incursions of armed bodies of marauders into the Nizam's territory, and, in the same year, was employed, under Brigadier Tomkyns, against insurgents at Shorapur.

In 1844 a troop was employed at Alur and, later on, in quelling a disturbance at Shorapur.

In 1845 a troop was engaged against a party of rebels under Musam Sahib at the village of Kulkunda.

In 1847 two troops, under Captain Macintire, were on service at Gumsur from February to May, and the left wing of the regiment was employed, under Captain Hampton, in the reduction of Fort Kandat.

In 1849 a wing of the 2nd Cavalry was, with Brigadier Hampton's force, despatched in the pursuit and capture of Appa Sahib, when two hundred of the enemy were killed or captured on the 6th May.

Another wing was employed, under Brigadier Onslow, during the same operations.

In 1850 a squadron was employed with Captain Wyndham's force in quelling disturbances at Malkapur.

In 1851 the 2nd Cavalry served under Brigadier Beatson at the siege of Dharur.

In March 1852 a detachment of the regiment, two hundred and fifty strong, was despatched to Man Resur, under Brigadier Mayne, to act against the Rohillas, and in December one hundred men were employed against the rebel Narsing Rao.

In 1853 Brigadier Mayne, with two hundred and sixty-six men of the regiment, suppressed the rebellion at other places in Berar.

In 1854 three hundred men were present at the siege and capture of Sailur.

In 1855 a squadron captured forty Rohillas at Darkingaon.

In July 1857 a detachment of the regiment took part in the defence of the Hyderabad Residency.

In 1858 forty troopers were engaged in the capture of Shorapur, co-operating with the Karnul column.

A squadron under Captain Macintire served with General Whitlock's force in Central India in 1857-58 and took part in the Battle of Banda.

A portion of the regiment served under Brigadier Hill in 1858-59 and was present at the action at Chichamba. The

Victoria Cross was conferred on Captain Clogstoun, 2nd Cavalry, for gallantry on this occasion.

In 1860 and 1861 detachments were employed in the pursuit of Rohillas in the Mahor and Nirmal jungles and at Chandur.

Captain Macintire was made a Companion of the Bath for his service in Central India.

In 1879–80 the 2nd Cavalry, under Captain Hamilton, was employed during the Rampa Rebellion.

It will be seen from this summary that the regiment had its full share of active service since its origin in 1816.

After the year 1880 the bands of Pindaris, Rohillas and Bhils had ceased to operate, and peace reigned over the land, though dacoits in certain districts were still active.

The regiment for the next thirty-five years resumed its life in cantonments in the Deccan. Individual Officers and men saw active service in different parts of the world, but during all this period the cavalry regiments were never far apart. They frequently met in Bolarum, at polo tournaments, shikar parties, and elsewhere.

The Hyderabad Contingent was a local corps with high traditions and a great *esprit de corps.*

We now come to the Great War, when the regiment was ordered to France at the end of 1914.

By the time it reached France, the stage of trench warfare had been reached, and therefore it was employed in relieving other units in the trenches, making raids in No Man's Land, digging new trenches in rear of the first line, and, when opportunity offered, doing what training it could, both mounted and dismounted. The horses had to be kept fit in whatever way was possible.

The horsemastership of the Indian cavalry during this period was always a source of wonder and admiration to the French and Belgians.

At Neuve Chapelle in March 1915 it was hoped that a sufficient gap would be made to let the cavalry through, but this did not materialize. At Loos they were again disappointed. Intensive trench warfare ensued and no opportunity occurred for cavalry to act in their proper rôle.

In July 1916 the Battle of the Somme commenced and the cavalry were warned to be ready to break through, but again the opportunity did not occur. Hope was again raised on the 9th November 1917 when the Battle of Cambrai was started, but by the 22nd November this new offensive came to an end.

The year 1918 started none too cheerfully, but General Allenby was planning the round-up of the Turkish Army in Palestine and in February orders were received for the regiment to proceed to Egypt.

It disembarked in April and, after two months' training in Palestine, marched in July to the Jordan Valley to defend the bridge-heads on the British right flank.

On the 19th September 1918 General Allenby launched his great offensive which for all time will stand out as a peerless example of using a large force of mounted troops. The results surpassed even the most sanguine expectations.

A few hours before the great advance started General Allenby assembled his generals and unit commanders at a place near the assembly position on the seashore (our left flank) and expressed the hope that 30,000 prisoners would be captured. The Desert Mounted Corps, in which this regiment was a unit, captured over 46,000 prisoners.

The great success of this advance was partly due to the fact that the enemy had hardly an aeroplane available to use against us. A great many had been shot down before the advance started and others destroyed at their aerodromes. We held complete mastery of the air.

A great many of the long marches were carried out in the daytime and there was no trouble from the skies. The regiment was lucky to have taken part in the most spectacular feat of the whole war. All the dreary days in France had not been wasted. It was worth waiting for this.

After the capture of Aleppo on 31st October 1918 the war in Palestine ended.

Much has happened since that date. Practically the whole of the British cavalry has been mechanized. Instruments of destruction have been invented which far surpass any imagination.

War now means the destruction of women and children in their houses, hundreds of miles from the scene of conflict.

Whatever the future may bring and whatever the rôle that the Indian cavalry may have to play, I feel sure it will always uphold those great traditions of which it may well feel proud.

Note.—Information as regards the early history of the regiment has been obtained from Major R. G. Burton's *History of the Hyderabad Contingent,* which is now out of print.

INTRODUCTORY NOTE

by

MAJOR SAWERS
29th Lancers (Deccan Horse)

THE War Diary of the 29th Lancers covers the period 10th August 1914 to 11th November 1920.

This abridged account has been written in order to preserve an accurate and readable record of the services of the regiment during the above period.

Much of the wording of the original diary has been retained and no attempt has been made to rewrite the actual account of actions written at the time in the field.

29th LANCERS, 1914-1920

1914

10th August.—Poona. A telephone message was received from the Brigade Major ordering the recall of all British Officers on leave in India. This was followed on the 13th August by the recall of all leave and furlough men.

26th August.—Mobilization orders received at 11.30 a.m. Mobilization for possible service with Indian Expeditionary Force " A."

2nd September.—Mobilization completed. The message to Divisional Headquarters read : " Mobilization completed and regiment ready to move."

During the period of mobilization squadron lines were evacuated and the men went into tents. The buildings were then used for storage purposes. The ten per cent. first reinforcements were obtained by demands on the 2nd Lancers, at Saugor, and on the 27th Light Cavalry.

Sixty-four horses, complete with saddlery, were received from these units.

15th September.—One extra blanket, extra flannel shirt, vest and drawers were issued, followed by the issue on the 10th October of warm serge clothing.

14th October.—Entrainment orders received, and the regiment moved in three trains to Bombay.

15th October.—Embarkation carried out : " C," " D " and H.Q. Squadrons in s.s. *City of Baroda*; " A " and " B " Squadrons in s.s. *Gregory Apcar*; 29 men and 30 horses of " C " Squadron in s.s. *Pundit*.

16th October.—During the day ships lay off the harbour. Rations for men and horses were drawn and found to be very good. At 6 p.m. all ships set sail.

16th October to 7th November.—During the voyage horses were exercised daily and kept very fit. Feeds at first consisted of 5 lb. bran and 3 lb. oats. This was changed on entering cooler weather at Port Said to 4 lb. bran and 4 lb. oats. The 12-lb. ration of Indian hay was found insufficient.

Two cases of staggers were treated by squirting the animals with a hose-pipe, and all fever cases were brought up on deck in the cool of the evening, which resulted in the lowering of temperatures.

29th October.—Suez reached.

31st October.—Port Said reached.

7th November.—Marseilles reached.

7th November.—Three squadrons disembarked and, after drawing new rifles on the quay, marched to camp at Parc Bareilly. " A " Squadron followed on the next day. It had been raining and the camp was under water.

During the first few days ashore it was found that the men's feet swelled from the cold, and as a result considerable difficulty was experienced in the proper fitting of boots.

An epidemic of mumps broke out in camp and by the 14th November there were twenty-two men in hospital and thirty-three in segregation.

10th November.—The regiment entrained for Orléans, travelling along the south of France and the Spanish frontier, reaching Orléans at midnight 12th/13th.

13th November.—Camp La Source was formed four miles from the station. There was heavy rain and the camp was found under water.

Here remounts and two machine guns were issued.

December.—On the 8th the regiment moved by rail to Haut Rieux, where billets were provided; all men under cover, but only forty per cent. of the horses in the first instance.

English-pattern horseshoes and some transport were issued in this camp, and training in route marching, trench digging and bomb throwing commenced.

25th December.—The Brigade was ordered to move towards Heuchin. Accordingly the 29th Lancers occupied Fontaines-les-Boulans and Fieffe. Here horse exercise, digging, and route marching were carried out.

1915

January.—The weather continued wet but not very cold when, on the 8th, a demand was received for a statement of available rifle strength to proceed to the trenches.

Reconnaissance parties went ahead, and on the 9th the dismounted regiment, 300 rifles strong, entrained for Béthune, which was reached at 4.30 p.m.

At 9 p.m. the regiment moved off with guides to relieve the 6th Cavalry in the trenches. "A" and "D" Squadrons were detailed for the front line, which was found three to four feet deep in water throughout its length. "C" Squadron went to the support trench; H.Q. and "B" Squadron to billets in the local reserve area. Owing to deep water the communication trenches could not be used, and positions were approached by the road. The light from two burning hayricks threw the men into strong relief and the regiment suffered fourteen casualties :—
Killed: No. 1402 Duffadar Arjun Singh and No. 1855 Lance-Duffadar Momchun Singh. Wounded: "A" Squadron, seven; "D" Squadron, five.

Conditions made the evacuation of wounded difficult, and the blanket stretchers were found to be very inefficient.

The machine guns during that night were useless owing to the quantities of mud which had entered the mechanism.

January, 1915.—On the morning of the 10th orders came that the regiment would keep up fire all day to support an attack to be carried out by a portion of the 1st Infantry Division. The telephone was broken so the message had to be sent under heavy fire by two orderlies* and arrived just in time.

In accordance with orders received, the firing line was evacuated and the support line occupied instead by 6.30 a.m. on the 11th January.

This was done as the support line was drier than the firing line. At 5.30 p.m. information was received that a jemadar† and four men were still in the original firing line and, having expended all their ammunition, were asking for orders. They were recalled at once.

The regiment was relieved by the 2nd Lancers at 8.35 p.m. on the 11th January and returned to billets. On the 15th January Rissaldar-Major Indar Singh was murdered by Sowar Sisram Singh, who himself committed suicide.

The regiment was inspected by the Prince of Wales in February.

March to May, 1915.—The regiment marched down for the Neuve Chapelle offensive on the 9th March, spending the night in the Bois des Dames, and then returned to billets in Estrée Blanche. On the 24th April the regiment marched via Hondechem to St. Jean-les-Bieman, and again on the 2nd May via Hondechem to Mametz and Crecque.

On the 27th May billets were again changed to camp at Vlamertinghe.

June, 1915.—On the 1st June Lieutenant-Colonel Saunders carried out a reconnaissance of bridges over the Ypres Canal, and

---

* No. 1799 Sowar Noor Ali and No. 2535 Sowar Rahman Khan II.
† Jemadar Hayat Ali Beg.

the regiment was ordered to be ready to move at half an hour's notice. There was heavy firing all day on the 2nd but no movement. Finally, at 7.40 p.m. on the 3rd, the regiment (dismounted) moved up to the rendezvous (Vlamertinghe crossroads) and was joined by the 36th Jacob's Horse. Thence they were led through Ypres, crossing the moat at Sallyport, to near Yeomanry Post. Masks had to be worn in the town owing to the presence of gas.

At 1.30 a.m. on the 4th they occupied G.H.Q. trenches (some very shallow trenches just west of Zillebeke Road), and at about 6 p.m. the regiment withdrew and returned to camp by Menin Road. Camp was shelled intermittently, and the Brigade returned to the Mametz area on the 15th.

July, 1915.—On the 8th July the Corps was inspected by Lord Kitchener. During this month large digging parties were at work in the First Army area, and Lieutenant-Colonels Pollard and Lillingston reported to War Office for orders. Lieutenant-Colonel Saunders was appointed officiating Commanding Officer and Major Cheyne appointed officiating Second-in-Command.

August, 1915.—On the 1st August the regiment marched via Senlis, Contre, Transu and St. Leger to Fieffe and Montrelet, arriving there on the 6th. On the 22nd the regiment marched to Forceville Wood, whence horses were brought back to billets, and on the following day the Lucknow Brigade trench party (the dismounted men) went into the support line at Authuille, whilst the Cavalry Division occupied the front line near Thiepval.

September, 1915.—Working parties were out daily, and the party was relieved on the 3rd September by the Secunderabad Brigade and returned to billets. From the 4th to the 12th of September large working parties were employed at Frechencourt, and on the 13th the trench party returned to the trenches at Authuille, going into the firing line on the 14th, in relief of 9th Hodson's Horse.

Trenches were heavily shelled during the evening and the party was relieved by the 7th Gordons on the 16th, having suffered eighteen casualties (four killed, fourteen wounded).

On the 21st September the Corps was inspected by Lord Kitchener.

On the 22nd September the 29th Lancers marched to new billets in Hardinval and Occoches, where two new Vickers machine guns were received and a second machine-gun section formed under Second-Lieutenant Falconer.

October to December, 1915.—On the 9th October billets were moved to Boisbergues and Authieux and again, on the 22nd, to Picquigny and St. Pierre-à-Gouy; then on the 18th November to Conde Folie and Eroile; and again, on the 21st November, to Conde Folie and Bettencourt. Finally the regiment moved to billets in Saigneville, in the immediate neighbourhood of which the whole Division was concentrated.

During the whole of this period the regiment was under training, with particular attention paid to the use of the bayonet and bomb. While at Saigneville, Divisional parades and sports were held, and in the latter the 29th Lancers were runners-up in the wrestling, being beaten by the Mhow Brigade.

1916

January, 1916.—During January the machine guns moved to Le Montant where they were brigaded with those of the King's Dragoon Guards and the 36th Jacob's Horse, to form the Machine Gun Squadron, to which, in the following month, Second-Lieutenants Mercer and Falconer were transferred.

March to May, 1916.—On the 26th March billets were changed to Fontaine l'Etalon and Cherienne, the 1st Indian Cavalry Division having been transferred to the Third Army.

May, 1916.—From the 9th to the 14th May the regiment

went out to Brigade training at Yvrench and Yvrencheux, returning to billets on the 15th.

On the 9th May billets were changed to Canettemont, and on the 24th "A" and "C" Squadrons moved to Estréewahin.

June, 1916.—On the 18th June a working party of six British Officers, 300 Indian ranks and four Hotchkiss guns, under Major V. K. Birch, was sent up to help in carrying stores and in tunnelling in the front line. The party returned on the 27th, having had four casualties (two killed, two wounded).

On the 25th June Woordie-Major Mohamed Umer Khan was murdered by Sowar Yad Ram.

On the 30th June billets were changed to Hilly, on the 2nd July to Villers Hôpital, and on the 19th July to Cahbligneul.

July, 1916.—On the 19th July, a working party of seven British Officers and 300 Indian ranks, under Lieutenant-Colonel Cheyne, went up to Aux Rietz (part of the labyrinth) and worked in the trenches by Neuville St. Vaast, returning to billets on the 31st July.

August, 1916.—On the 1st August the regiment went back to billets in the training area at Chelers, Le Tirlet and Herlin-le-Vert.

On the 7th August Lieutenant-Colonel A. R. Saunders proceeded to take up a special appointment in Marseilles and Lieutenant-Colonel Cheyne to command the 18th Durham Light Infantry; while Major P. B. Sangster, D.S.O., 2nd Lancers, assumed command of the regiment.

On the 9th billets were changed to Warlincourt-le-Pas. From the 10th to the 14th a working party of seven British Officers and 377 Indian ranks, under Major C. G. H. Henderson, were at Squastre, and worked nightly in the front line by Fonquevillers. From the 15th to the 20th a patrol under Lieutenant Rice, with Jemadar Natha Singh and seven other ranks, were at Bienvillers carrying out reconnaissances in No Man's Land.

On the 21st billets were changed to Warluzel. On the 29th a working party of four British Officers and 150 Indian ranks, under Major H. Meynell, proceeded to Bienvillers, returning on the 2nd September.

September, 1916. — On the 3rd September the regiment marched via Outrebois to Domvast, and on the 11th via Bealcourt-Milly to Querrieux, arriving there on the 13th and going into bivouac. The Division was concentrated here.

On the 15th the regiment marched to bivouac at Dernacourt. From here patrols under British and Indian Officers were sent up daily to Leuze and Delville Woods to reconnoitre the route. On the 26th the regiment marched via Ledaours, Mametz, Bussy, Hangest, Bellancourt to Machie, arriving there on the 30th.

During September the dismounted men were collected divisionally and employed chiefly in making cavalry tracks up to Leuze and Delville Woods. On the 25th Captain E. W. Spurgin, who was in charge of the dismounted men, was wounded. This party rejoined on the 1st October.

October, 1916.—During October the regiment remained in billets at Hachiel and Caumartin, doing schemes with troops daily — Divisional, Brigade, Regimental and Squadron exercises being practised. On the 2nd November billets were changed to Chepy and Acheux. The regiment remained here under training.

The Machine Gun Squadron went up dismounted on the 20th October, 1916, to the trenches on the Ancre. They had a fairly quiet time at first but subsequently took part in the attack of the 13th November on Beaumont Hamel and Serre.

November, 1916.—The Lucknow Machine Gun Squadron, under Captain A. A. Mercer, was attached to the 31st Division (93rd Brigade) and went into the line at the foot of the Serre

Ridge, with four guns in the front line and four in support; it remained in the line twenty-seven days without relief. On the opening of the attack on the 13th November Lieutenant J. F. Falconer was severely wounded when holding an advanced post with his section, but refused to leave duty and remained with his guns till he was carried away exhausted. He was afterwards awarded the Military Cross.

During this battle Captain A. A. Mercer was ordered to send two guns out to an advanced post which was to be held at all costs till our attacking troops were back in their original line. This was done and the post held for sixteen days. On leaving the trenches the Lucknow Squadron was thanked by the G.Os.C. 93rd Brigade and 31st Division, who said that the gallantry of the sections in sticking to their positions had undoubtedly saved the 93rd Brigade from being surrounded and probably captured.

December, 1916.—After seventy-two hours' rest the Squadron had four more days in the line and then returned to its own Brigade.

On the 12th December Lieutenant-Colonel P. B. Sangster, D.S.O., was reported by a medical board as unfit to return from leave, and the command of the regiment devolved on Major V. K. Birch.

1917

January, 1917.—On the 21st January the men who had been with the Machine Gun Squadron returned, having been replaced by British personnel.

For a year the Brigade Machine Gun Squadron had been composed of men from the three regiments in the Brigade.

February, 1917.—On the 15th February Lieutenant-Colonel P. B. Sangster, D.S.O., rejoined from sick leave and resumed command of the regiment. On the 27th February the regiment marched via Kaours to Henencourt.

March, 1917.—On the 2nd March a working party of two British Officers and 254 Indian ranks proceeded to Bazentin-le-Petit under Lieutenant Follit. The following day Major G. W. Hemans relieved Lieutenant Follit, who rejoined the regiment, and on the 4th March Major G. W. Hemans was killed in action. Major G. Marchant then took over command of the digging party.

On the 15th March the regiment marched to new billets in Bonneville and Canaples. On that day the regiment left Bonneville at 12 noon, arriving at Henencourt Wood at 4.30 p.m. On the 16th H.Q., "A," "B" and "C" Squadrons were placed under II Corps and "D" Squadron under I Anzac Corps. "A," "B" and "C" Squadrons carried out reconnaissances by officers' patrols under Captain Jackson, Captain Wright and Major Marchant respectively.

"A" Squadron patrol marched to Loupart Wood.
"B" Squadron patrol marched to Grevillers.
"C" Squadron patrol also marched to Loupart Wood via Le Sars and Warlencourt.

The remainder of the regiment remained in bivouac.

At 10 a.m. on the 17th the regiment was parading for inspection by Lieutenant-General Sir W. Birdwood, commanding I Anzac Corps, when orders were received for the regiment, less one squadron, to march at once to the north-eastern outskirts of Le Sars, and the 29th Lancers were, by the same order, placed under the orders of the 2nd (Infantry) Division, with Headquarters at Courcelette.

At 12 noon the regiment left Henencourt Wood, arriving at Le Sars at 3.30 p.m., where it was met by the Officer Commanding who had received instructions to bivouac in Aqueduct Road. A message was sent back to Lieutenant

Clarke, in charge of "B" Echelon, ordering him to halt at Ovillers-la-Boiselle, as the regiment might be withdrawing there next day. The horses were unsaddled and preparations commenced to bivouac when, at 4.30 p.m., orders were received from the 2nd (Infantry) Division to move up to Loupart Wood and thence east of Bihecourt in the direction of Ervillers with patrols to gain touch with the enemy, who might be retiring from Achiet-le-Grand and Logeast. Lieutenant Mercer was sent on to reconnoitre a route through the wire and shell-pitted area.

At 5.15 p.m. the regiment marched for the north-western corner of Loupart Wood. "A" Echelon, under Lieutenant Gavaghan, was directed to move via Pis to the north of Loupart Wood, and thence to follow the regiment towards Bihecourt. "C" Squadron was detailed as advanced guard.

At 5.30 p.m. orders were received from the 2nd Division to march on Mory as well as Ervillers and to endeavour to establish positions in these two villages. In consequence "C" Squadron was ordered to reconnoitre from Bihecourt towards Gommiecourt, with patrols also towards the Bois de Logeast. "A" Squadron was directed to reconnoitre by Behagnies towards Ervillers and Mory, with "B" Squadron in reserve. The task of crossing the wire and shell-pitted area was accomplished with the loss of but two pack animals, which could not be extricated from shell holes into which they fell. At 6.30 p.m. "C" Squadron arrived at the south-eastern corner of Bihecourt, which had been evacuated by the enemy and was then being intermittently shelled. Patrols were pushed out as directed, but were held up immediately by machine-gun fire. As it was getting dark the regiment bivouacked for the night south-west of the railway line just south of Bihecourt when, at 8 p.m., orders were received to withdraw immediately to Le Sars. As it was quite dark and very difficult to cross the shell-pitted area in the dark, the Commanding Officer decided to lead horses back via Irles and Pis and the regiment arrived at Le Sars at 1 a.m. on the 18th.

At 4.10 a.m. on the 18th information was received that Bapaume, Achiet-le-Petit, Bienvillers and part of the Bois had been captured, and the Lucknow Cavalry Brigade would move to Achiet. The 29th Lancers were replaced under the orders of the Lucknow Cavalry Brigade, with orders to move as advanced guard to the Brigade. In accordance with this "C" Squadron was detailed as vanguard with orders to secure the high ground west of Gommiecourt, with patrols into Gommiecourt and towards Ervillers. "A" Squadron was ordered to secure the high ground south-west of Courcelles, with patrols into Courcelles, and to reconnoitre the eastern edge of the Bois de Logeast, and towards Ablainzeville. "B" Squadron, on arrival at Achiet-le-Grand, to send a patrol towards Behagnies. Messages were sent to :—

(1) Lieutenant Gavaghan to move via Irles to join Brigade "A" Echelon (one troop of "B" Squadron sent as escort);
(2) Lieutenant Clarke to move and rejoin Brigade "B" Echelon on the Albert–Aveluy Road.

At 6 a.m. the regiment marched to Bihecourt via the north-western corner of Loupart Wood, reaching Bihecourt at 7.30 a.m., whence patrols were sent out, and the march continued to Achiet-le-Grand, where Headquarters arrived at 9 a.m. Shortly afterwards "C" and "A" Squadrons respectively reported Gommiecourt and Courcelles clear of the enemy.

At 10.15 a.m. orders were received for Headquarters and "B" Squadron (less one troop) to join Brigade Headquarters half a mile north of Achiet-le-Petit, which was accordingly done. At 11.55 a.m. "C" Squadron reported Ervillers clear of the enemy and held by one troop; shortly afterwards "A"

Squadron reported holding Hamelincourt with one troop. About this time the Brigade moved under the shelter of the Bois de Logeast and watered and fed.

At 3.25 p.m. orders were received that the Brigade would move in a north-easterly direction. "A" and "C" Squadrons rejoined the main body of the Brigade (less one troop of each left in Hamelincourt and Ervillers respectively until relieved by infantry of the 7th and 62nd Divisions). "C" Squadron brought in one prisoner.

At 5 p.m. the regiment arrived at Y roads, half a mile west of Gommiecourt. "D" Squadron rejoined the regiment, also "A" and "C" Squadrons (less one troop each). At 6 p.m. the Brigade moved forward to the railway between Gommiecourt and Ervillers and bivouacked for the night.

At 5.30 on the 19th the Brigade continued to advance in a north-easterly direction, the 29th Lancers being in reserve. At 9 a.m. "A" Squadron troop rejoined from Hamelincourt, having been relieved by infantry. At 12 noon the Brigade advanced to under Mory Ridge, which was being shelled intermittently at the time. At 3.45 p.m. the Brigade withdrew into the valley east of Ervillers and bivouacked there later. "B" and "D" Squadrons were on outpost duty that night.

At 5.30 a.m. on the 20th March verbal orders were received (confirmed in writing at 6.50 a.m.) that the 6th/5th Northamptonshire Regiment would attack Croiselles at 7 a.m., and that the Lucknow Cavalry Brigade would co-operate; the 29th Lancers, with two sections of Hotchkiss guns, would protect the left flank of the infantry advance on the west of Croiselles by securing the high ground north-west of that village, with patrols towards Menin. Two troops to be left on the high ground between Judas Farm and the Ervillers Road, with patrols towards Boyelles and Boiry, in order to obtain touch with the infantry.

In consequence Headquarters and "C" Squadron moved

to St. Leger at 6.50 a.m. " B " Squadron was recalled from the outpost line and ordered to follow up. " D " Squadron (leaving two troops holding the outpost line) rejoined the regiment near St. Leger. " A " Squadron had been despatched to Achiet-le-Grand to draw rations, and was ordered to return as soon as possible.

At 7.30 a.m. the Commanding Officer, with " C " Squadron, arrived at St. Leger and, seeing that a squadron of the 36th Jacob's Horse had crossed to the north of the railway and was then halted on the south-eastern slopes of the high ground around St. Leger, directed Major Marchant to take his Squadron up and report to Major Maunsell, who was presumed to be in command of the 36th Squadron.

At the same time the Commanding Officer went off to confer with the infantry Colonel with a view to ascertaining how the regiment could best help the left of the infantry advance. Thereafter the Commanding Officer went to get in touch with Majors Marchant and Maunsell (36th Jacob's Horse), who were presumed to be at the Moulin.

The Commanding Officer got in touch with Major Marchant on the high ground between the Moulin and Croiselles, where Major Marchant and Major Meynell (who had come up in the meantime with two troops of his squadron) had gone forward to reconnoitre. These officers came under machine-gun fire from Croiselles, but eventually rejoined the Commanding Officer. The General Officer Commanding joined the Commanding Officer here at 9 a.m. and ordered the regiment to cover the left of the infantry attack on Croiselles and to push the attack on the west and north sides of that village.

To cover this movement two sections of machine guns which had joined the regiment were ordered to secure, as a pivot, the high ground north of St. Leger, with one troop of " D " Squadron as escort. At 9.15 a.m. Major Marchant's squadron, acting as advanced squadron, pushed forward patrols to the high ground west and north-west of Croiselles, backed up by the remainder of the squadron, with a view to securing that position preliminary to further operations against the west and north of Croiselles. The remainder of that portion of the regiment which had then been able to concentrate from the outpost line held on the night 19th/20th and a squadron of the 36th Jacob's Horse, moved to the valley, one mile east of Boyelles, in support of the advanced squadron.

Major Marchant's squadron got held up by machine-gun fire from the ridge just north-west of Croiselles. Meanwhile information had been received that the infantry attack on Croiselles had been held up midway between St. Leger and Croiselles and could not proceed. Seeing that the infantry attack had been held up, that a patrol of the regiment had reported Menin still held by the enemy, and that the line between Menin and Croiselles appeared to be strongly held, the Commanding Officer decided to make a further reconnaissance of the enemy's line before committing the regiment.

At 10.30 a.m. he withdrew the two groups of "D" Squadron and the squadron of the 36th Jacob's Horse, which were being shelled in the valley — the latter to rejoin its own regiment in Brigade reserve, the former to the cover of the railway embankment north of Judas Farm. Major Marchant's Squadron was ordered to hold the high ground around the Moulin de St. Leger with two sections of Hotchkiss guns and to continue pushing forward patrols to the west and north-west of Croiselles to keep touch with the enemy.

Meanwhile "B" Squadron had been collected from the outposts and moved up to the cover of the railway embankment, north of Judas Farm, and at 10.45 a.m. "A" Squadron rejoined from Achiet-le-Grand, where it had gone to draw rations. At this hour the regiment and two sections of Hotchkiss guns were disposed as follows: One squadron with four Hotchkiss guns holding the Moulin de St. Leger; three squadrons with Headquarters under cover of the railway embankment north of Judas Farm. This position for the reserve was considered a good one:—

> (a) As forming a good jumping-off place for further operations between Menin and Croiselles should the patrols of the advanced squadron report any weakening of the enemy's lines;
> (b) As being convenient for supporting the advanced squadron;
> (c) As furnishing excellent facilities for observation;
> (d) As being well protected by the embankment from artillery fire;
> (e) As filling a gap between the infantry (whose left flank the 29th Lancers had been protecting) and the 2nd/4th London Regiment, which had now come up on the left flank of the regiment and with whom touch was gained.

In the course of the day the Northamptonshire Regiment, on the right of the 29th Lancers, was relieved by the 8th Devons.

At 11.30 a.m. one Squadron of the 36th Jacob's Horse was sent in support of the 29th Lancers and was held in reserve near the small wood half a mile south of St. Leger. Continual reconnaissances by patrols were pushed out throughout the day towards the line Croiselles–Menin, both in order to maintain touch with the enemy and to get estimates of his strength, while "D" and "B" Squadrons were sent in turn to Achiet-le-Grand for rations, returning as quickly as possible, the latter bringing "C" Squadron's rations as well as its own.

The position remained thus until 6 p.m., when Headquarters and "B" Squadrons moved to the small wood just south of St. Leger to relieve the squadron of the 36th Jacob's Horse (which returned to its own regiment) and to bivouac for the night.

"D" Squadron was left under cover of the railway embankment and ordered to patrol every two hours after daybreak towards Menin and between Menin and Croiselles, while "A" Squadron was sent to relieve "C" Squadron and hold the Moulin de St. Leger and to push dismounted patrols towards Croiselles and mounted patrols to the west and north of that village, so as to keep touch with the enemy.

"C" Squadron then rejoined Headquarters and bivouacked for the night.

During the day Captain Spurgin rejoined, having been absent since the 18th carrying out reconnaissance work for the I Anzac Corps.

On the 21st "A" and "D" Squadrons continued patrolling all day, the rest of the regiment staying in bivouac until 4 p.m., when a brigade of artillery came up, requiring the position for their batteries. Headquarters, "B" and "C" Squadrons then withdrew and bivouacked in the valley east of Ervillers.

At 10.35 p.m. "A" Squadron was relieved by the Border Regiment, but continued patrolling duties until daybreak on the 22nd, when the 36th Jacob's Horse took over patrol duties from both "A" and "D" Squadrons.

The regiment remained in bivouac till the morning of the 26th and then marched to Aveluy, where "A" and "B" Echelons rejoined.

April, 1917.—On the 8th April the regiment marched to Irles and on the 10th moved to a position of readiness in accordance with a plan previously circulated to Commanding Officers in connection with an attack by the Fifth Army on the Hindenburg Line.

At 7.30 a.m. a snowstorm came on and, owing to the

postponement of cavalry operations, the regiment was ordered to march back to Irles at once.

At 2.45 a.m. on the 11th April it again moved up to the same position of readiness and off-saddled. In the evening a snowstorm came on which continued throughout the night, and on the 12th the regiment marched back to Irles, and on the following day to Aveluy and thence to Louvencourt.

From here "A" and "C" Squadrons proceeded to Bussy-les-Artois, the remainder of the regiment following on the 18th. During the month information was received that Captain C. V. Martin (Temporary Lieutenant-Colonel) attached Headquarters Staff, X Corps, had been killed in action on the 27th March 1917.

May, 1917.—On the 15th May the regiment marched via Meaulte and Suzanne to le Mesnil, and on the 24th to Hamelet.

On the 29th a detachment of the regiment, under Captain M. H. Jackson, M.C., relieved a similar detachment of the 2nd Lancers for work on the Brown Line and also as a reserve for the front line. The enemy shelled the spot for two hours on the evening of the 31st, and in consequence the working party was moved to a new position near Templeux.

June, 1917.—During the night of 3rd/4th June the detachment relieved the 38th Central India Horse in Posts 8-13, B3 Subsector.

At 9 a.m. on the 4th the details left in camp marched (under Major G. Marchant) to St. Christ, taking over the camp vacated by the 2nd Lancers.

The detachment under Captain Jackson, M.C., passed a quiet day. Patrols were sent out, but were held up by enemy covering parties.

On the 5th the enemy shelled Posts 11 and 12 during the afternoon. On the 7th heavy rain fell, necessitating a considerable amount of work in the trenches.

On the 10th heavy rain fell, making the fairway of the trench very bad and causing the parapet to fall in in many places. Second-Lieutenant Clarke took out a patrol from No. 11 Post along Enfilade Trench. His patrol was challenged after proceeding a short distance and Second-Lieutenant Clarke fired at the sentry, who shouted " Kamerad, don't shoot," and then threw bombs at the patrol, wounding Lieutenant Clarke and one non-commissioned officer.

Lieutenant Follit was then sent out but could not get in touch with the enemy. Lieutenant Falconer, M.C., at the same time took a patrol out from Post No. 9 to ascertain if Cologne Farm were held. After covering three-quarters of the distance he was held up by about twenty Germans and was unable to proceed further, and was himself slightly wounded.

On the 11th, at 9.30 p.m., the enemy opened a violent trench-mortar bombardment on No. 9 Post, with three heavy *minenwerfers*. This bombardment lasted about an hour. Captain Spurgin, who was standing by for wiring, was then ordered to take his party and commence work round Post No. 9. No sooner had he started than the bombardment reopened on this post and lasted another hour. A short time afterwards the enemy made an attack on Post No. 9—about fifty Germans being engaged therein—which was successfully driven off.

The following is an extract from a report by Lieutenant-Colonel Wickham, commanding B3 Subsector: " I saw the whole of the bombardment from Battalion Headquarters and I consider that the greatest credit is due to the troops employed in the defence of No. 9 Post and Lieut. Rice who was in command, for their behaviour during a trying time. I consider it all the more creditable as most of the men employed had not been subjected to a bombardment of heavy T.Ms. before, and the fact that two if not three were being employed against them made it all the more trying. The way they beat off the attack with rifles and Hotchkiss Rifles was excellent. I wish to bring to your notice the names of the following officers: Lieutenant R. A. Rice, Rissaldar Kabul Singh."

On the night of 13th/14th the wiring round No. 9 Post was practically completed. At 3.40 a.m. on the 14th the Germans made a very determined attack on No. 9 Post. Extract from report by Lieutenant-Colonel Wickham, commanding B3 Subsector: "At 3.40 a.m., just as the advanced posts had been withdrawn from the E. and S. of Unnamed Farm, a party of the enemy about 30-40 strong were seen to be approaching. Rifle and Hotchkiss Rifle fire was at once opened on them. The enemy replied with volleys of rifle grenades and rushed up to the wire on the south side of No. 9 Post, covered by the fire of three Machine Guns. At the same time another party, of about the same strength, was seen advancing from the east from New Trench. They were held up by our wire and Captain Spurgin at once attacked them, moving out through the wire, and drove them out. He himself was wounded and three of his men killed. Another party of the enemy was seen coming up from New Trench, north of the cross roads, by men in No. 11 Post. Hotchkiss Rifles were turned on to them and they retired. By 5.30 a.m. the attack had been driven off. I consider that in view of these most exceptional circumstances the garrison of No. 9 Post did particularly well in driving off this most unexpected attack. The strength of the enemy is estimated at about 80-90 supported by three Machine Guns. One of the defenders' Hotchkiss rifles was knocked out almost at once by a rifle grenade. I should like to bring to your notice the names of the following officers for exceptionally good work during this attack and in the previous one on the night of 11th/12th: Captain Jackson, Captain Spurgin, Lieutenant Rice, Rissaldar Kabul Singh."

During the night 15th/16th the detachment was relieved

by the 38th Central India Horse and went back to advanced Divisional Headquarters at Hervilly, where they received some reinforcements, and on the night of 16th/17th the refreshed detachment took over B2 Subsector, under the command of Major R. J. H. Baddeley, M.C., with Headquarters at Fervaque Farm.

On the 17th Lieutenant-Colonel Sangster took over the command of B2 Subsector. Fervaque Farm was shelled daily.

At 3 a.m. on the 22nd the enemy opened a trench-mortar bombardment on No. 6 Post. At 4.30 Captain Mercer located the trench mortar and two batteries opened fire on it, when the bombardment immediately ceased.

During the night of 25th/26th Lieutenant J. F. Falconer, M.C., took a patrol to the German line at Quarry Trench. He found a gap in the wire and entered the trench, in which he found no enemy. He then took the patrol on to the second belt of wire in front of Farm Trench. The patrol endeavoured to cut their way through this wire to get into the trench. The wire was very thick and of great depth, and day began to break before a gap had been cut. Lieutenant Falconer therefore brought the patrol back to our lines, having encountered no enemy; but having seen and heard them in Farm Trench.

On the night of the 28th/29th Ressaidar Badlu Singh took a patrol to the same place as that reconnoitred by Lieutenant Falconer above, with the same result.

On the night of 29th/30th the detachment was relieved by the 17th Lancers and marched back to Hamelet (less one platoon under Lieutenant Follit sent to Hervilly). On the 30th the remainder of the regiment joined the detachment at Hamelet.

July, 1917.—On the 5th July the regiment marched to Le Mesnil and passed into Corps Reserve.

On the 23rd a dismounted working party under Lieutenant G. D. Baines proceeded to join a dismounted brigade from the

4th Cavalry Division (attached to the 34th Division). Copy of an address given by Brigadier-General H. F. Gage, D.S.O., commanding Lucknow Cavalry Brigade, to the 29th Lancers on a parade on the 4th July 1917 : " The G.O.C. wishes to take this opportunity of congratulating the 29th Lancers on its good work and steady conduct while in the trenches. In this respect he particularly wishes to express his admiration at their gallant behaviour during the period 3rd to 15th June, when two determined attacks were made by the enemy on Post No. 9 which was garrisoned by ' A ' Squadron. In the first attack, the garrison withstood a severe bombardment by heavy trench mortars with exemplary steadiness, and when the enemy advanced, expecting to find the garrison had retired, he was quickly driven back by that portion of the garrison which had not become casualties. On the second occasion, a surprise attack was attempted, covered by volleys of rifle grenades, but the 29th Lancers had again to be reckoned with, and the attack was equally unsuccessful. Similarly the bold spirit animating the patrols of the 29th Lancers is worthy of special commendation. On one occasion a patrol sent towards Cologne Farm succeeded in reaching the enemy's wire and in bringing back valuable information in spite of a barrage of bombs which was hurled at them. On another occasion a patrol penetrated the enemy's line in Quarry Trench, and on finding this unoccupied, advanced to the enemy's second-line trench and endeavoured to cut a way through the wire only being prevented from doing so by the approach of dawn.

" The above incidents show that all ranks of the 29th Lancers are imbued with a resolute, determined and fighting spirit, worthy of its traditions, and in congratulating all ranks on their gallantry in action, the G.O.C. wishes to add that he is more than ever proud to have such a magnificent regiment under his command.

" He particularly wishes to mention the following names for exceptionally good work.

"Duffadar Puran Singh, Sowar Sunder Singh, Acting Lance-Duffadar Bishen Singh, Lance-Duffadar Sham Singh, Duffadar Indar Singh, Sowar Arjan Singh, Acting Lance-Duffadar Kehar Singh, Sowar Daya Singh, Sowar Kartar Singh, Sowar Kehar Singh, Sowar Hari Singh, Lance-Duffadar Chet Singh, Sowar Nikka Singh, Sowar Indar Singh, Acting Lance-Duffadar Sundar Singh, Sowar Mall Singh, Lance-Duffadar Kishen Singh, Acting Lance-Duffadar Jaimal Singh, Lance-Duffadar Indar Singh, Sowar Nahar Singh, Sowar Indar Singh, Acting Lance-Duffadar Ralla Singh, Acting Lance-Duffadar Dasounda Singh, Sowar Khazan Singh, Lance-Duffadar Shib Dayal, Sowar Bhoran Singh, Sowar Ramji Lall, Lance-Duffadar Chainchal Singh, Sowar Sis Ram."

August, 1917.—On the 5th August an advance party proceeded by lorry to Epéhy and reported to Brigade Headquarters, 104th Infantry Brigade, whose left battalion was to be relieved in the trenches by the Lucknow dismounted detachment. At 9 p.m. the advance party proceeded to Battalion Headquarters, 20th Lancashire Fusiliers, in the sector opposite Honnecourt.

On the 7th, arrangements for the relief were completed, with the King's Dragoon Guards in the front line, the 36th Jacob's Horse in reserve and the 29th Lancers in support.

On the night of the 9th/10th Lieutenant Falconer and Second-Lieutenant Sawers took a patrol out to see if Crawford Crater were occupied or not. They found it unoccupied and took the patrol on to the south-western corner of Honnecourt Wood, where they were met with machine-gun fire and bombs were thrown at them. Lieutenant Falconer then withdrew his patrol.

On the night of the 10th/11th Lieutenant Follit took a patrol to the southern edge of Honnecourt Wood, a little to the east of the patrol of the previous night. He saw two Germans, but established the fact that some outlying posts were not held by the Germans and that two rows of wire marked on the map did not exist.

On the nights of the 11th/12th and the 12th/13th patrols went out to Honnecourt Wood and on the latter night cut the wire with a view to entering the trench on the following night.

During the evening of the 13th a local relief was carried out, the 29th Lancers taking over the firing line from the King's Dragoon Guards. Working parties had been provided nightly up to this night, but now that the regiment held the front line, they were no longer required.

During the night of the 13th/14th a patrol (Lieutenant Follit) entered and searched the post, the wire of which had been cut on the previous night; but it was found to be unoccupied, though a large working party was heard in Honnecourt Wood. Another patrol (Second-Lieutenant Sawers) went right up to the German wire at Les Tranchées, when it was challenged and fired at heavily, causing it to withdraw. Two patrols went out again on the night of the 14th/15th.

On the 15th the regiment was ordered to change places with the battalion on its right, and on the night of the 16th/17th the 29th Lancers were relieved by the 19th Lancers and went into local support behind the 36th Jacob's Horse in the front line of the new sector.

At 4 a.m. on the 19th the infantry on the right attacked and captured the Knoll and Guillemont Farm, but the 29th Lancers did not become involved, and on the night of the 19th/20th the regiment was relieved by the 17th Lancers,

Fusiliers, and the 23rd Manchesters, and marched back to Saulcourt, where they were met by led horses and reached Le Mesnil at 10 a.m. on the 20th.

At 3.30 p.m. on the 21st a dismounted detachment, under Captain Jackson, M.C., proceeded to Vendelles and took over the right half of the firing line and supports, the King's Dragoon Guards being on the left and the 36th Jacob's Horse on the right.

On the 22nd and 23rd the front line was shelled and five casualties sustained. Two patrols went out nightly. On the nights of the 23rd/24th and 24th/25th they were held up by machine-gun fire. On the night of the 24th/25th Lieutenant Rice was wounded. On the night of the 28th/29th the 29th Lancers were relieved by the 36th Jacob's Horse and went into reserve. Casualties during this period were one killed and four wounded.

September, 1917.—On the 2nd September an enemy deserter reported that a raid was contemplated on the night of the 2nd/3rd and so the 29th Lancers moved up into the support line, but nothing occurred; and on the night of the 3rd/4th the 29th Lancers were relieved by the 19th Lancers and returned to Le Mesnil.

On the 12th September an advance party under Major Henderson left for the front line and were followed by a dismounted detachment on the following day. The trench party went into reserve, taking over Morval Trench on the right bank of the Omignon river, the left bank being held by the French.

On the night of the 20th/21st the trench party took over the left subsector from the 36th Jacob's Horse, occupying Lone Tree Post and Dragoon Post in the firing line, with the Fort Garry Horse and Hodson's Horse respectively as support and reserve posts.

On the night of the 20th/21st Lieutenant Follit with "B" Squadron Platoon and two Hotchkiss guns occupied Somerville Wood. At about 12.50 a.m. a German patrol attacked this standing patrol, but was driven off and one prisoner was captured. On the night of 21st/22nd "D" Squadron Platoon found the standing patrol in Somerville Wood, and Lieutenant Follit with a patrol lay up at Max Bank; small enemy patrols were seen, but there was no contact.

On the night of the 22nd/23rd a patrol of "A" Squadron under Captain Wright, lay up on Max Bank and "B" Squadron found the standing patrol in Somerville Wood.

On the 23rd, "D" and "B" Squadrons relieved "A" and "C" Squadrons in Dragoon Post and Lone Tree Post respectively. On the night of the 23rd/24th "C" Squadron occupied Somerville Wood and "A" Squadron provided a wiring and covering party in that place. Somerville Wood was occupied by one non-commissioned officer and six men by day, and on the 24th a German patrol of twenty other ranks, under an officer, attacked this post at dusk, before the night patrol took over, but were driven off and one prisoner was captured. On this day the patrol was provided by "C" Squadron under Duffadar Abdul Rahim Khan, and "A" Squadron Platoon provided the standing patrol in Somerville Wood.

On the night of the 25th/26th "C" Squadron took over Somerville Wood and an "A" Squadron patrol, under Second-Lieutenant Harvey, proceeded to Max Bank, where they lay up. At 1 a.m. Germans were reported from the direction of Eleven Trees. At 1.10 a.m. a large party of the enemy approached Max Bank and Second-Lieutenant Harvey, who was on the flank at the time, gave the order to charge. He was almost immediately knocked down by a bomb and slightly wounded. Jemadar Rur Singh took command. After this encounter the enemy's patrol withdrew towards his lines and our patrol returned to Somerville Wood with one British Officer and three other ranks wounded.

On the 26th the daily arrangements for the occupation of Somerville Wood were altered with a view to enticing the enemy further forward. It was known that he was anxious to obtain an identification in this part of the line. Consequently " B " Squadron, under Lieutenant Follit, took up a position near the centre of Somerville Wood, supported by " C " Squadron under Lieutenant Herrick, just in advance of Lone Tree Post. The patrol came under heavy rifle-grenade fire from the direction of Max Bank, three other ranks being wounded.

On the night of the 27th/28th the same patrols occupied Somerville Wood as on the previous night, but no enemy was seen. At 8.30 a.m. on the 28th the enemy shelled Somerville Wood, wounding one other rank. Two strong patrols from " D " and " C " Squadrons lay up in Somerville Wood, as on the previous night, but no enemy were seen.

On the 30th the trench party was relieved by the 3rd Rifle Brigade and returned. During this period the casualties were eight wounded.

October, 1917.—On the 2nd October a party of forty-four other ranks proceeded to Devise Camp, where winter lines and stables were being prepared for the Division. On the 5th two Indian Officers and 100 Indian other ranks, under Lieutenant Falconer, joined the hutting party at Devise, and on the 8th another party of one Indian Officer and eighty Indian other ranks, under Lieutenant Follit, joined.

During the month the following was published : " The G.O.C. has much pleasure in publishing the following names which have been brought to his notice for good work in the trenches during the period 24th May to 30th September 1917. The names of those who have already received awards are not republished.

"Ressaidar Daya Singh, Jemadar Jaisi Ram, Jemadar Gulab Singh, Duffadar Puran Singh, Duffadar Indar Singh, Lance-Duffadar Sham Singh, Acting Lance-Duffadar Sunder Singh, Sowar Sundar Singh, Sowar Arjan Singh, Sowar Rattan Singh, Sowar Daya Singh, Sowar Kartar Singh, Sowar Kehar Singh, Sowar Nika Singh, Sowar Indar Singh, Sowar Surta Singh, Duffadar Mehoo Singh, Sowar Alakh Ram, Sowar Ram Chander, Duffadar Pirthi Singh, Duffadar Jai Lall, Lance-Duffadar Lalji Singh, Sowar Khazan Singh, Duffadar Abdul Rahim Khan, Lance-Duffadar Mohammed Hafiz, Acting Lance-Duffadar Mohammed Hussain, Acting Lance-Duffadar Kutab Ali."

November, 1917.—On the 11th November, 1917, the regiment moved into the new lines at Devise. On the 9th two British Officers (Captain Bradley and Lieutenant King), four Indian Officers and eight Duffadars proceeded as advanced party to join the 4th Cavalry Pioneer Brigade and were followed on the 15th by the remainder of the party, consisting of sixty other ranks. This party was employed solely in preparing the cavalry track for the impending attack (Battle of Cambrai).

On the 19th November the regiment marched from Devise to Longavesnes, where the night was spent under canvas. On the 20th they marched to Heudicourt. A patrol of one troop under Lieutenant O'Connor was sent on ahead to co-operate with the infantry and gain touch with the enemy, with the object of finding out whether Grèvecourt was held by the enemy. At 1.25 p.m. the regiment, still leading the Brigade, marched from Heudicourt and camped for the night on either side of the cavalry track, near the Hindenburg support line. At 9 p.m. Lieutenant O'Connor returned and reported Grèvecourt and the bridge over the canal strongly held by the enemy.

On the 21st the regiment moved back to low ground south-west of La Vacquerie. A patrol of six men, under Jemadar Mahbub Ali, was sent out to reconnoitre the road and approaches to Grèvecourt, returning at 5.30 p.m. and reporting that place held, having come under machine-gun fire on the Gouzeaucourt–Bon Avis Road.

At 5.30 p.m. the regiment marched to Fins, and bivouacked for the night. On the 23rd, at 8.15 a.m., the regiment, at the head of the Brigade, marched via Nurlu and Doingt to Devise. At 5 a.m. on the 25th the regiment marched, at the head of the Brigade, via Vraignes and Roisel to Villers Faucon, and in the evening returned to Devise, reaching there at 5 p.m.

At 11.5 a.m. on the 30th the regiment marched, at forty minutes' notice, to a position of concentration, and at 5 p.m. left the Brigade, with orders to report to the Officer Commanding the 6th Queen's, at Vaucelette Farm. On arrival there, at 7.45 p.m., orders were received to report to the General Officer Commanding the Canadian Cavalry Brigade, from whom, at 10 p.m., orders were received to rejoin the Lucknow Brigade, in accordance with which the regiment rejoined the Brigade at 1.20 a.m. When about to move the regiment came under indirect machine-gun fire and Ressaidar Newal Singh was killed and one other rank wounded.

December, 1917.—At 3.30 a.m. on the 1st December the regiment marched to a point of assembly, where the whole Brigade dismounted and led horses were sent back to the former position under Captain Jackson, M.C.

Orders were received directing the regiment to act as Brigade reserve in a dismounted attack on Villers-Guislain in conjunction with tanks, and in consequence the regiment moved forward to a position of readiness. Owing to the non-arrival of the tanks, the attack did not take place, and the regiment remained here till 3.30 p.m., when it moved up about five hundred yards, to the vicinity of the railway, as Brigade reserve to an attack by the 36th Jacob's Horse and Jodhpur Lancers on the Raperie. Two squadrons occupied a trench and two were in the railway cutting west thereof. The advanced squadrons were in touch with the infantry on the left, but there was no infantry in touch on the right. Patrols were consequently pushed out to gain touch. Owing to the non-arrival of the Mhow Brigade to cover the right flank and the fact that the Raperie was strongly held, the advanced regiments did not succeed in gaining their objective and the 29th Lancers were ordered up to fill the gaps in the line on both flanks.

This was carried out with " C," " A " and " D " Squadrons in the firing line and " B " in support. At 4 a.m. the following morning the regiment was relieved by a battalion of the Durham Light Infantry and moved back before dawn to a rear position where, at 5.45 a.m., it joined the remainder of the dismounted Brigade.

At 2 p.m. orders were received that Lucknow Brigade dismounted personnel were to be organized into a dismounted battalion under Lieutenant-Colonel Holden, and consequently the 29th Lancers were organized into a dismounted company under Major Marchant. Lieutenant-Colonel Sangster, the Adjutant, Signalling Officer, and certain Headquarters personnel, rejoined the led horses, which had been moved to bivouac just north of St. Emilie.

At 4.30 a.m. on the morning of the 3rd the dismounted company also rejoined, having passed an uneventful period as part of the Lucknow Brigade, in reserve to the Sialkot Brigade.

At 8.30 a.m. the regiment marched via Roisel, Vraignes and Mons to Le Mesnil. On the 13th the Brigade was inspected by the General Officer Commanding and the rapid formation of the dismounted battalion practised. On the 17th the regiment marched to former lines at Devise.

On the 25th a working party proceeded to Jeancourt for work under the C.R.E., returning the same evening; a similar party proceeded the following day for three days' work on Le Verguier switch, and another party of the same size for a day's work under the C.R.E., and again on the 29th. It is interesting to note that the regiment was employed in strengthening Le Verguier, which held out longest when the Germans attacked this part of the line in 1918.

1918

January, 1918.—From the 1st to the 5th and from the 12th to the 24th working parties were sent daily to Jeancourt or Bihecourt. These parties, consisting of 100 men under a British Officer, were employed in constructing and repairing the defences in the neighbourhood of Le Verguier.

On the 26th January an advanced party, under Major V. K. Birch, proceeded to Hesbecourt and were followed on the next day by a trench party, under Major R. J. H. Baddeley, M.C. They remained in huts at Hesbecourt, in reserve, providing daily working parties, of one hundred, on the front line by night and twenty on stables at Montigny Farm by day.

February, 1918.—On the 5th February the trench party took over a sector of the front line with "A," "B" and "C" Squadron platoons in the front line and "D" in support. Mer, Marten and I, V and Y Posts were shelled lightly each day. Patrols were sent out by night, but nothing of particular note occurred, and on the 8th the trench party were relieved and returned to Hesbecourt. Here working parties continued as before until the 13th, when the Brigade trench party was relieved by the 24th Division. In the meantime the regiment, less trench party, had marched from Devise to the Namps-au-Mont area, and the trench party rejoined here on the 14th.

On the 22nd February 7 British Officers, 3 British other ranks, 8 Indian Officers and 402 Indian other ranks, under Lieutenant-Colonel P. B. Sangster, D.S.O., entrained at Saleux in three trains for Taranto, *en route* for Egypt, while on the 5th March the regiment, less dismounted party, entrained at Saleux in three trains for Marseilles.

March, 1918.—The advanced dismounted party sailed from Taranto on the 10th March, reaching Tel-el-Kebir without incident on the night of the 15th/16th. The regiment sailed from Marseilles in three boats. The first party—on S.M.T. *Hyperia*—sailed on the 15th and reached Tel-el-Kebir on the 2nd April. The voyage took sixteen days and septic pneumonia broke out on board amongst the horses and, as there were nearly seven animals to one man on board, the casualties were heavy—seventeen animals died and seventy were evacuated immediately on landing.

The remainder of the regiment—on H.T. *Volumnia* and H.T. *Kingstonian*—left Marseilles on the 19th in the same convoy and reached Tel-el-Kebir on the 29th March without incident.

During the autumn and winter of 1917-18, immediately previous to the regiment's arrival in Egypt, the Egyptian Expeditionary Force had made a successful advance, resulting in the capture of Beersheba on the 31st October 1917, Jaffa on the 16th November, Jerusalem on the 9th December, and Jericho on the 20th February 1918, and thereby advancing the line practically to where it remained until September 1918.

The moral ascendancy reached by the British was such that the following remarks occur in a letter written by a German Staff Officer as early as the 21st November 1917: "We have had a very bad time. After having had to relinquish good positions which have been held for so long (Gaza—Beersheba), the breakdown of the Army is greater than ever I could have imagined. But for this complete dissolution, we should still be able to make a good stand at Jerusalem. Now the VII Army bolts from any cavalry patrol." On the 21st March a special force, known as Shea's Group, from its Commander, carried out a raid on Es Salt and Amman, involving the difficult crossing of the Jordan under fire at a time when, owing to the rains, it was unfordable. On the 2nd April the force returned west of the Jordan after hard fighting, leaving the 180th Brigade to form a bridge-head on the east of the river at El Ghoraniye.

A second raid was undertaken on the 29th April. The object of this raid was to co-operate with an advance of Sherifean troops on Es Salt; but the latter failed to appear and our troops were again withdrawn west of the Jordan by the 4th May. These two raids did much to convince the enemy that the ultimate advance on Damascus would be made by Es Salt and Amman, with Deraa as a primary objective. This compelled him to keep his Fourth Army east of Jordan and his forces thus divided into two groups, separated by a difficult obstacle—the Jordan river and valley. Such was the situation when the regiment joined the Egyptian Expeditionary Force.

April, 1918.—The regiment marched from Tel-el-Kebir on the 16th April, reaching Kantara on the 17th, and thence entrained for Belah on the 21st, where they went into camp and remained there under training till the 4th May, on which date the regiment left Belah and marched to Jericho in six stages, with a day's rest at Talaat-ed-Dumm, reaching Jericho on the 15th.

May, 1918.—On arrival there the 8th Mounted Brigade, of which the 29th Lancers formed a part, passed into the Divisional Reserve of the 1st Mounted Division, which took over the right sector of the Jordan front from the Dead Sea (exclusive) to El Auja (exclusive).

On the 17th May the regiment relieved the Mysore Imperial

Service Lancers, for patrolling duties. These consisted of two troops out beyond the wire by day, with patrols, at irregular intervals, towards the foothills, to obtain touch with the enemy, and two troops out beyond the wire by night, to prevent enemy parties approaching unobserved within two miles of our wire. These patrols were found in turn by each Squadron. Contact with the enemy was established daily, but nothing beyond patrolling occurred. Working parties were at work on communications in the area from the 18th to the 24th.

On the night of the 30th/31st the 8th Mounted Brigade were relieved by the 6th Mounted Brigade and passed into Divisional Reserve, the 29th Lancers being relieved by the 2nd Lancers. During this month the regiment took eighteen prisoners and lost one Indian other rank missing.

June, 1918.—On the 7th June the regiment relieved the 36th Jacob's Horse and took over the line from the Dead Sea (exclusive) to El Ghoraniye bridge-head (exclusive) with Headquarters at Ain Hajla. Two posts were held, X Post covering El Henu Ford, and Y Post covering the fords of Hakhadet Hajla and Kasr-el-Yehoud, both these posts being west of the river. Patrols continually moved along the rest of the front, from and between these posts.

During the period from the 8th to the 12th a pontoon bridge was constructed across the Jordan at El Henu. The actual work of building the bridge was carried out by Royal Engineers personnel, but eight working parties were provided by the regiment and much of the preliminary reconnaissance for the site. The preparation of the crossings of the Wadi Rame was also carried out by the regiment. At this part both banks of the Wadi Rame and the eastern bank of the Jordan were covered with very dense, tall rushes to a depth of ten to thirty yards. While these provided good cover from view, they formed a serious obstacle to the preliminary reconnaissance.

The bridge was completed by the 12th and in consequence a small bridge-head on the east bank of the Jordan was formed and held by one troop from the garrison of X Post.

In this connection the following letter was received from the Headquarters of the 18th Mounted Brigade: "The Brigade Commander wishes to express his appreciation of the success with which you have conducted the bridging of the Jordan river at El Henu. The previous reconnaissance, which involved much labour, was thorough and efficient; whilst the crossings which you have prepared over the Wadi Rame have been extremely well executed, and should, it is hoped, contribute largely to the success of future operations."

On the evening of the 13th, the London Yeomanry relieved the regiment in all positions except that on the east bank of the river at El Henu.

During the night "C" Squadron, under Captain Spurgin, M.C., and "A" Squadron, reinforced by two troops of "D" Squadron, under Captain M. H. Jackson, M.C., the whole under Lieutenant-Colonel P. B. Sangster, D.S.O., crossed the Jordan at El Henu and worked up the east bank of the Wadi Rame to Ford 1125. Here the detachment halted until dawn. At dawn "C" Squadron, in line of troop columns, with "A" Squadron echeloned back on the right, advanced towards Tel Ghussul. After proceeding in this formation for about three-quarters of a mile, rifle fire was opened from Tel Ghussul, and "C" Squadron charged from the left and "A" Squadron from the front. The position was captured and one Turkish Officer and eight men taken prisoner, while seven Turks were killed with the lance. "C" Squadron then worked south and crossed the Wadi Ghuer. On being fired on heavily from the foothills by machine guns, the Squadron turned right handed and recrossed the Wadi Ghuer lower down, then, keeping the Dead Sea on its left, returned to El Henu. Meanwhile "A"

Squadron, in support, swept the intervening country, but no signs of the enemy were found. Both Squadrons recrossed the Jordan on the 14th and "B" Squadron were then relieved by the London Yeomanry, and the regiment again passed into Divisional reserve at Jericho. The following day Lord Allenby came down to congratulate the regiment on being the first to get their lances into the Turk in the Jordan Valley. On the 16th, in connection with an operation to be carried out by the 6th and 8th Mounted Brigades, the regiment took over the Ain Hajla sector from the London Yeomanry. These two Brigades carried out a demonstration on the morning of the 17th, but the regiment did not become involved in any active operations, and on relief that day returned to camp near Jericho.

On the 21st the regiment again relieved the 2nd Lancers in the El Ghoraniye bridge-head and remained there, carrying out the usual patrolling duties until the 8th July, when they were relieved by the 20th Deccan Horse and marched out of the Jordan Valley. Between the 10th May and the 8th July the regiment had captured fifty prisoners.

July, 1918.—During this period Lieutenant R. S. King was sent out with a small patrol to investigate the operations of an enemy working party, who were protected by a covering party. Coming under heavy rifle fire from the latter he promptly charged the enemy and dispersed them, killing some and capturing two prisoners.

On the evening of the 8th the regiment marched via Talaat-ed-Dumm and Enab to Latrun, reaching the latter place on the 11th. All marches were made by night to avoid the heat.

On the 23rd the regiment marched to Zernuka and remained there under training till the 10th August. On the 30th July General Sir E. Allenby, Commander-in-Chief of the Egyptian Expeditionary Force, inspected the Division.

August, 1918.—On the 10th August the regiment marched

back to Jericho, arriving there on the 14th. On the 15th the regiment relieved the 20th Deccan Horse at the bridge-head, moving into camp west of the Jordan and taking on patrol duties, as before, east of the Jordan.

On the 21st August a fire was seen and a patrol of the 29th Lancers, under Lieutenant R. L. W. Herrick, was sent forward to investigate. They proceeded up the Wadi Nimrin and reported "two men standing near a fire." Lieutenant Herrick then made a reconnaissance and saw eighteen men. He thereupon despatched two men to attack them from their rear and himself charged with four men. The enemy, on seeing him, opened fire and started to retire towards the foothills, firing all the while, but on being charged from their rear, surrendered, throwing their arms down. Heavy, but inaccurate, machine-gun fire was then opened by four machine guns from the foothills, and also shrapnel and high explosive. The prisoners were collected into three parties and marched down the wadi, followed by artillery fire as far as the day post. Two Sowars were sent back to collect some of the rifles, but owing to heavy machine-gun fire, could only bring away three. Total capture: Eighteen Turkish soldiers of the 1st and 3rd Battalions 191st Regiment, 48th Division, of whom five were wounded with the lance. One of the prisoners stated that the crops were being burnt to prevent their men deserting and our own from collecting forage.

On the 28th General Sir G. Barrow visited the regiment and conveyed to Lieutenant Herrick and the patrol the congratulations of the Commander-in-Chief and announced the following immediate awards for the patrol encounter of the 21st August, 1918 :—

Distinguished Service Order : Lieutenant Herrick.
Indian Order of Merit : Duffadar Jot Ram.

Indian Distinguished Service Medal : Sowar Karam Singh, Sowar Imrat Singh, Sowar Mool Singh, Sowar Ram Dayal, Sowar Ghasi Ram.

September, 1918.—The regiment remained at the bridge-head and continued to carry out patrolling duties until the 10th September. During this period the Hotchkiss guns were reorganized, the four guns of each squadron being collected into a separate Hotchkiss Gun Troop. This change was fully justified by the events which had occurred previously and which followed in the advance of September, 1918.

On the 11th September the regiment was relieved, the 20th Indian Infantry Brigade taking over the night outpost duties, while the 6th Australian Light Horse took over the patrolling duties, and on the 11th it marched out of the Valley via Talaat-ed-Dumm to Junction Station, arriving there on the 14th. Thence the regiment proceeded to Ramleh on the evening of the 15th. On the 16th and 17th all unnecessary kit was dumped and ordnance stores drawn to complete equipment. On the 17th the regiment marched to Selme, where the 4th Cavalry Division was concentrated for the battle about to commence.

On the 19th September, at 4.30 a.m., the XX and XXI Corps attacked the enemy along the whole front held by these two Corps, the artillery bombardment starting at the same moment as the infantry attack, and in a very short time the infantry were through the enemy trench system at several points.

The 7th Indian Division cleared a way for the cavalry, and at 8.30 a.m. the 4th Cavalry Division received orders to advance, the 11th Cavalry Brigade leading, with the 36th Jacob's Horse in advance and the 29th Lancers in rear of the Brigade. No opposition was encountered and the enemy's line was crossed about 10 a.m., the trenches, which were not deep, having been filled in by a Divisional Pioneer party.

The Ramadan Marsh was crossed at 11 a.m. by the Zerkiyeh crossing, and at 12.45 p.m. Burj-el-Atot was reached without incident. Here the Brigade fed, and at 1.30 p.m. the advance was continued. The Tul Keram–Kakon–Liktera line was found unoccupied and, with the exception of one small party, no opposition was encountered throughout the day. At 4.45 p.m. Tel-ed-Dhrur was reached and the Brigade watered and fed. Meanwhile Beidus and Kerkur were captured, after slight opposition, by the 12th Brigade.

At 9.15 p.m. the march was continued, the order of march being: the 2nd Lancers, the 12th Brigade, the 11th Brigade, the 10th Brigade (less the 2nd Lancers). The Musmas Pass was negotiated successfully during the night and the regiment debouched on to the famous plain of Armageddon at El Lejjun (the Meghiddo of the Bible) at 7.15 a.m. on the 20th. Here, on reaching the plain, the 2nd Lancers had met with some enemy, killing or capturing the whole party. At El Lejjun the whole Division watered and fed, the 10th Brigade then being pushed on to Afule.

While at El Lejjun "C" Squadron was detailed to act as escort to Divisional Headquarters, and one troop (fifteen lances) under Lieutenant King, M.C., seeing a large body of enemy cavalry, charged them, killing or capturing the whole party, the number of prisoners being 4 Officers and 144 other ranks.

At 9.15 a.m. the regiment marched to Afule as advanced guard to the Brigade, arriving there at 11.15 a.m., and relieved the 10th Brigade, which then proceeded towards Beisan. At Afule "C" Squadron rejoined the regiment, which fed and halted till 3 p.m., when the Brigade (now in rear of the Division) marched for Beisan, the 29th Lancers being advanced guard.

The first parties, retreating northwards, from the Seventh and Eighth Turkish Armies, now began to make their appearance, and the regiment captured 2 German other ranks, 14 Turkish Officers, 325 Turkish other ranks, and one machine gun, all without opposition.

At 8 p.m. the regiment arrived at Beisan and camped for the night, the 10th Brigade providing the outposts. The regiment stood to at 4.30 a.m. on the 21st, but as all was quiet stood down again at 5.45 a.m.

Parties retreating from the Seventh and Eighth Turkish Armies now appeared in great numbers, and at 6 a.m. " B " Squadron was sent to hold the Valley of Jezreel, from Afule (exclusive) to Beisan (exclusive), to prevent stragglers escaping northwards, while one troop of " D " Squadron, under Lieutenant Ashton, was posted south of Beisan to assist the Brigade outposts line. At 5 p.m. " D " Squadron troop was withdrawn, while the 5th Cavalry Division took over the Valley of Jezreel as far as Shutta, the line Shutta (inclusive) to Beisan (exclusive) being held by " A " and " B " Squadrons, under Major Baddeley, M.C., during the night of the 21st/22nd. No fighting took place, but 2 German other ranks, 1 Austrian other rank, 97 Turkish other ranks and 6 Arabs were captured during the twenty-four hours.

The two Squadrons in camp stood to for an hour at dawn, and at 6 a.m. " A " and " B " Squadrons were relieved by the London Yeomanry and returned to camp.

During the day the 12th Cavalry Brigade took over the outpost line from the 10th Cavalry Brigade, and as one regiment of the former Brigade was detached, the 29th Lancers were attached to it and placed in reserve. At 6 p.m. one troop of " D " Squadron took over the policing of Beisan village, and at 7 p.m. the remainder of the Squadron was sent to assist the Staffordshire Yeomanry, south of the village, who were unable to cope with the large number of prisoners coming in. The number of prisoners taken during the day by the regiment, excluding those escorted by "D" Squadron, was forty-eight other ranks.

On the 23rd September "D" Squadron was relieved of all duties, and rejoined. Information now having been received that large parties of the Turkish Seventh and Eighth Armies were escaping eastwards across the Jordan, the 11th Cavalry Brigade was ordered to move southwards to cut off any such parties and with a view to eventually joining up with the Anzac Division for an advance along the western bank of the river.

In accordance with this plan the Brigade marched south, the 36th Jacob's Horse on the eastern bank of the river and the main body of the Brigade on the western bank. The regiment formed the advanced guard to the main body of the Brigade, with "C" Squadron as vanguard.

Khan-es-Sumariyeh village was reached without opposition, but on the arrival there of the main body of the Brigade information was received from the Officer commanding the vanguard that his left troop was held up by machine-gun and rifle fire from a considerable body of enemy cavalry and infantry in a position south-east of the village and between it and the river. "A" and "D" Squadrons, under Captain M. H. Jackson, M.C., were then sent to deal with the situation.

A personal reconnaissance by Captain Jackson revealed the fact that a large body of Turkish troops was endeavouring to make good its escape across the ford to the south-east of the village, covered by a strong rearguard, which was the party which had fired on "C" Squadron and was also holding the ford on both sides of the river with machine guns.

The position held was an extended one. Captain Jackson therefore detached "A" Squadron to work round the right flank of the enemy towards the river, while he himself, after putting "D" Squadron's Hotchkiss guns into a position from which he could bring effective fire to bear on the enemy, made a wide circling movement round the enemy's left flank with the remainder of the Squadron, and charged the position from the rear. In spite of very heavy fire the charge succeeded and over 1,000 Turks, including a Divisional General, were captured with 18 machine guns and 12 automatic rifles. "D" Squadron's casualties were, however, heavy.

Meanwhile, hearing the heavy firing, the Commanding Officer took "B" Squadron to assist, if necessary, but the Squadron arrived on the scene after "D" Squadron's charge was over. "B" Squadron was then sent on towards the ford, but being received with very heavy fire could not get home and took up a position facing the ford. During this operation Captain R. D. Wright was wounded. Part of "B" Squadron was then sent to join "A" Squadron, and Major R. J. H. Baddeley took command of both and worked his Hotchkiss guns down the right bank to bring fire to bear on the enemy machine guns. In the meantime "D" Squadron returned into Brigade reserve, its Hotchkiss-gun troop shortly afterwards being sent forward to help "C" Squadron, which reported a large body of Turks advancing from the south. This party, however, surrendered without fighting.

As the enemy crossed the river eastwards, he withdrew his machine guns, "A" and "B" Squadrons' Hotchkiss troops following them up and firing with good effect. By 12.30 p.m. the west bank of the river was clear of the enemy, though the east bank was still held by him, but by 2.30 p.m. the enemy had retired and the ford was held by one troop of "B" Squadron. At 3.5 p.m. touch was gained with the 36th Jacob's Horse on the eastern bank of the river, and at 4 p.m. "A" Squadron was sent with that regiment to advance down the eastern bank of the river to join the London Yeomanry, a squadron of which was being sent forward to cross by a more southerly ford. At 5 p.m. the Brigade continued its advance southwards and halted for the night just north of Ras-el-Humeiyir. The London Yeomanry found the outposts, hence "C" Squadron and "D" Squadron Hotchkiss-gun troops rejoined. Captures by the regiment during the day were large: 2 German Officers and 50 other ranks, 75 Turkish Officers and 2,250 other ranks were counted; and it is probable that the actual numbers considerably exceeded 3,000, while 21 machine guns and 12 automatic rifles were also taken. The regiment's casualties during the day were:—

>Killed in Action: Rissaldar Badlu Singh and seven other ranks.
>
>Wounded: Captain R. D. Wright, Jemadars Dale and Jaidall Ram and fourteen other ranks.

Immediate Awards :—

>Distinguished Service Order: Captain M. H. Jackson, M.C.
>
>Military Cross: Jemadar Jailal.
>
>Indian Order of Merit (1st Class): Duffadar Dharam Singh.
>
>Indian Order of Merit (2nd Class): Sowar Jitu Singh, Sowar Balwant Singh, Sowar Mukam Singh, Sowar Bhagwan Singh.
>
>Indian Distinguished Service Medal: Sowar Nikka Singh.
>
>Victoria Cross (posthumous): Rissaldar Badlu Singh.

On the 24th Major R. J. H. Baddeley, M.C., rejoined with "B" Squadron, "A" Squadron rejoining shortly afterwards. At 10.30 a.m. information was received, by aeroplane, that about three thousand Turks were marching eastwards for a ford a little farther south. The Brigade therefore marched south with a view to intercepting the retreat of the Turks. The regiment proceeded at the head of the Brigade, with "D" Squadron as advanced squadron.

The enemy was found debouching on to the plain and was at once attacked, under cover of gun-fire, but his advanced troops had already reached the ford and considerable numbers succeeded in crossing to the east, where, however, some of them were captured by a squadron of the London Yeomanry which had been sent across by a more northerly ford the day before. Many others were captured by the regiment. Considerable casualties were also inflicted by our guns and machine guns, especially the latter, while the ford was being crossed. "A" Squadron's Hotchkiss guns also found good targets.

The fight continued, with the Brigade pushing the enemy south and east till, at 2.30 p.m., the regiment was holding the road to the El Ashert Ford. The Brigade then halted, and, as no more enemy were known to be about, proceeded down to the Jordan river and camped for the night. On the way down Lieutenant King, M.C., rejoined with his troop, having successfully passed right through the retreating enemy during the night and obtained touch with the Worcestershire Yeomanry at Khan Atuf, as ordered. Our captures were estimated at 900, but no accurate count was kept. Two machine guns were also taken.

The Brigade stood to as usual at dawn on the 25th, and as no more retreating Turks were reported by our aeroplanes, started to return to Ras-el-Humeiyir, but on the way orders were received from the Division to return at once to Beisan. The destruction of the Turkish Seventh and Eighth Armies was now complete, with the exception of the small bodies which had escaped east of the Jordan. Information having been received that these bodies were retiring on Deraa, together with the Turkish Fourth Army from the Es Salt and Amman area, with a view to escaping towards Damascus, the 4th Cavalry Division was directed on Deraa, to co-operate with the Sherifean troops in an endeavour to cut off this army, or follow it up if it had already escaped. At the same time the Australian and 5th Cavalry Divisions were directed on Damascus by the El Kuneitra Road from the west and north sides of the Sea of Galilee.

In accordance with this plan the 11th Cavalry Brigade marched from Beisan at 1 p.m. Jisr Mejame was reached at 5.30 p.m., where the 36th Jacob's Horse provided outposts for the night. During the day Captain E. W. Spurgin, M.C., was evacuated sick. On the 27th the march was continued to Irbid without incident, the Brigade marching at 8 a.m. and arriving at Irbid at 5 p.m. One troop of "B" Squadron, under Lieutenant J. C. J. O'Connor, was sent from Jisr Mejame via Umm Keis to serve as a flank guard and to gain information of the enemy. This rejoined at Irbid, having seen no enemy, but reporting that the latter had blown up the railway bridges east of Semakh. The 29th Lancers provided the outposts, but the night passed without incident.

One troop of "D" Squadron, under Lieutenant Ashton, was detached to administer the village of Irbid, and the Brigade, less this troop, marched on the 28th for Er Remite, where the Division was to concentrate for an attack, if necessary, on Deraa. Er Remite was reached at 8.30 a.m. and the Brigade watered and fed. Deraa was, however, found to have been evacuated and burnt, and the Division therefore proceeded to advance towards Damascus, and Mezerib was reached at 5.30 p.m.

On the 29th the Brigade was at the head of the Division with the 36th Jacob's Horse as advanced guard. No opposition was met *en route*, but desultory shooting by Arabs took place all day. Arriving at Dilli at 4.30 p.m., the Brigade bivouacked for the night.

On the 30th the Brigade continued its march on Damascus, the 29th Lancers forming the advanced guard. Desultory shooting at patrols by Arabs occurred all day, but nothing of particular interest until, at 7 a.m., a body of the enemy, 500 strong, was reported holding the ridge west of Mahaje. It subsequently transpired, however, that this was a body of Sherifean troops operating on our right flank. At Ghabaghib the Brigade watered and fed, and at 2.30 p.m. orders were received for the advanced guard to halt, the regiment being then about half-way between Zerkiyeh and El Haj.

The intention had been for the Division to reach Kiswe by evening and camp there; but it now appeared that this was impossible, hence at 3 p.m. orders were received to reconnoitre Jebel-el-Mania. If this were found free of enemy the Brigade would halt for the night at Khan Denun. If, however, it were held by the enemy, then the Brigade would halt for the night in the neighbourhood of Khiyara.

On receipt of these orders "B" Squadron was directed on Khan Denun with patrols to Kiswe Station on the Hedjaz railway. Under cover of this reconnaissance "C" Squadron was directed on Jebel-el-Mania, while the mainguard moved towards Khan Denun. "C" Squadron, in moving across the Ard-el-Khiara, came under artillery fire from a body of Turks, estimated at 1,500 strong, in the foothills north of Deir-Ali. About 5.30 p.m. our guns opened on the enemy and orders were received for two squadrons to be sent in support of "B" Squadron, which was reported to have headed off the Turks on Jebel-el-Mania. The Commanding Officer took "A" and "D" Squadrons to the grove west of Khiara Ghiftlik and was reinforced there by two machine guns.

Eight Hotchkiss guns and two machine guns were then pushed up about two miles towards the foothills, while "A" and "D" Squadrons moved on their left flank with a view to heading off the enemy. Owing to darkness, however, and the difficult nature of the country, the enterprise was abandoned about 7 p.m. and the regiment camped for the night on the west of the Khiara Ghiftlik grove. During this operation Lieutenant J. C. J. O'Connor was wounded. Throughout the day the going was very bad, the lava formations and boulders being exceedingly tiring to the horses' feet.

The total casualties since the regiment left Selme on the 19th now amounted to:—

> Killed in Action: One Indian Officer, nine Indian other ranks.
> Wounded: Two British Officers, two Indian Officers, seventeen Indian other ranks.
> Evacuated Sick: One British Officer, twenty-six Indian other ranks.
> Animal casualties were fifty-seven.

October, 1918.—On the 1st October the march towards Damascus was continued. The Brigade reached Sbeinat at 1 p.m. and halted there. By this time the Australian Mounted Division and the 5th Cavalry Division had arrived, the latter being on the foothills west of the town and the former to the north of Damascus, which was thus surrounded, except on the east, and entered on the 2nd October.

On the 2nd the regiment marched to the neighbourhood of El Judeide in order to be near the Kuneitra–Damascus Road, along which supplies must come. A march through Damascus of representatives from each unit took place during the day. Each regiment in the Brigade sent one squadron, the whole being under the command of Lieutenant-Colonel P. B. Sangster, D.S.O. The squadron from the regiment was made up of one troop from each squadron under Captain M. H. Jackson, M.C.

On the 5th Lieutenant Ashton and his party rejoined from Irbid, and on the same day Captain Jackson was evacuated sick. On the 6th, at 8.30 a.m., the regiment marched to El Hame. On the march the General Officer Commanding was evacuated sick and Lieutenant-Colonel P. B. Sangster, D.S.O., assumed command of the Brigade, the command of the regiment devolving on Major R. J. H. Baddeley, M.C.

On the 7th the regiment marched to Khan Meijloun, whence Lieutenant Follit was evacuated sick, and died in hospital a few days later.

News having been received that Rayak was in the hands of the 5th Cavalry Division, the 4th Cavalry Division, less one brigade, marched to Zebdain. On the 12th and 13th the march was continued via Et Tekkie to Bar Elias, where Colonel Sangster rejoined and resumed command. With a view to a further advance all led horses, with a minimum number of men to look after them, were transferred to a Divisional Details Camp at Shtora, the remainder of the regiment being organized into two squadrons. The numbers thus detached were Lieutenant R. A. Rice, M.C., Lieutenant R. L. W. Herrick, D.S.O., three Indian Officers, 75 Indian other ranks, 244 horses. The remainder of the regiment marched to Baalbek. On the 18th General Sir G. de S. Barrow inspected the horses of the regiment and remarked on the good turn-out of the men—" Horses satisfactory considering circumstances." On the 26th some warm clothing was issued, and on the 27th the regiment marched back via Bar Elias and Khan Meizebun to Damascus, reaching there on the 29th and bivouacking in the enclosure of the Australian Reserve Hospital. On the 31st forty Turkish prisoners were received to assist in bivouacs and news was received of the armistice between Turkey and the Allies.

The total evacuations during October had been: 7 British Officers, 3 British other ranks, 6 Indian Officers, 207 Indian other ranks, 6 followers, 36 animals.

November, 1918.—On the 13th November Lieutenant Ashton and Lieutenant King were evacuated sick. During the month three parties of reinforcements arrived from the base and the details which had been left behind in Shtora rejoined. On the

13th December Lieutenant-Colonel P. B. Sangster, D.S.O., took over temporary command of the Brigade, the command of the regiment devolving on Major R. J. H. Baddeley, M.C.

1919

January to April, 1919.—On the 7th January two Indian Officers and two Indian other ranks proceeded to Mecca as guests of the King of the Hedjaz.

On the 24th, 25th and 26th February the regiment moved by train to Semakh, taking over patrolling duties from the 5th Australian Light Horse.

On the 3rd April, Major Baddeley having proceeded on leave to India, the command of the regiment devolved on Captain M. H. Jackson, D.S.O., M.C.

On the 4th April " B " Squadron, under Captain R. L. W. Herrick, D.S.O., marched to Jerusalem to be under orders of the 8th Infantry Brigade to quell any disturbances during the festivals. On the 21st the regiment marched via Jisr Mejame and Irbid to Deraa, reaching there on the 23rd. On the march one troop, under Lieutenant G. B. Jackson, was detached at Irbid to keep order there and " D " Squadron, under Lieutenant T. Y. Hawkes, was left in Er Remite to protect the crops of that place from the Bedouins.

On the 24th " A " and " C " Squadrons, accompanied by the G.O.C. 11th Cavalry Brigade and the Political Officer, carried out a reconnaissance in force to the south of Er Remite.

On the 27th " A " Squadron, under Captain R. A. Rice, M.C., proceeded to reconnoitre at Nasib and to protect the crops and water supply from the Bedouins. On the 30th " C " Squadron relieved " D " at Er Remite.

May, 1919.—On the 6th May " D " Squadron relieved " C " at Er Remite, and Lieutenant-Colonel Sangster took over command from Captain Jackson. On the 7th " B " Squadron rejoined from Jerusalem. On the 9th "C" Squadron, under Lieutenant C. M. O. Sawers, marched to Tiberias, as trouble was expected in that area. On the 10th "A" and "B" Squadrons rejoined. On the 18th, Lieutenant-Colonel Sangster having proceeded on leave, the command of the regiment devolved on Captain M. H. Jackson, D.S.O., M.C. On the 20th "B" Squadron relieved "D" Squadron at Er Remite, and on the 25th and 26th respectively, "C" and "B" Squadrons rejoined.

June, 1919.—On the 15th June two troops of "D" Squadron proceeded for detachment duty to Es Salt and Amman. On the 23rd "A" Squadron, under Captain R. A. Rice, M.C., marched to Semakh.

July, 1919.—On the 1st July one Indian Officer, one non-commissioned officer and one Indian other rank were despatched to the United Kingdom to participate in the peace celebrations.

October, 1919.—On the 18th October the regiment, less "D" Squadron, marched to Semakh.

November, 1919.—On the 2nd November a patrol of twenty Indian ranks, under Captain M. H. Jackson, D.S.O., M.C., proceeded to reconnoitre a route to Tyre, returning on the 5th, the route chosen having been found to be impossible. On the 11th the regiment marched to Beisan, returning to Semakh on the 16th. On the 18th a patrol, under Lieutenant T. Y. Hawkes, proceeded to make a reconnaissance of the road Safed–Hule–Tyre and returned by train from Haifa on the 28th. The patrol carried out its reconnaissance, buying all supplies on the road and crossing the "Ladder of Tyre" on the way. On the 29th two troops of "D" Squadron rejoined from Deraa and two troops at Amman marched to Ghoraniye.

December, 1919.—On the 1st December Major E. M. Nixon, 36th Jacob's Horse, arrived and took over command of the regiment. On the 28th a patrol of thirty-six Indian ranks, under Captain R. L. W. Herrick, D.S.O., proceeded to reconnoitre the villages of Es Shunemaad and Es Sakhni, where large bodies of Bedouins were reported, but none were found, and the patrol returned on the 29th. On the 31st the following wire was received from the Brigade: " Military Governor Tiberias reports Abu Bassa held by Bedouins, send two strong Squadrons to clear up the situation." In accordance with this, " A " and " B " Squadrons, under Captain Herrick, D.S.O., marched at 2.30 a.m. on the 1st January, accompanied by two cars of the 7th Light Armoured Car Patrol. On nearing Abu Bassa they were fired on by a party of Bedouins, thirty to forty strong, occupying the foothills towards Midras. They opened a brisk fire from Hotchkiss rifles and drove the Bedouins farther into the hills. Being unable to cross the frontier the squadrons then withdrew and returned to Semakh. The Military Governor later reported that several Bedouins had been killed.

1920

January, 1920.—On the 7th and 10th January strong patrols again visited Abu Bassa. From the 11th to the 20th daily patrols proceeded to reconnoitre Esh Shuni, Maad, Abu Bassa, Berbera and El Adeise. During this month a barbed-wire apron was erected round the camps, and from the 2nd February an inlying picquet was posted nightly with patrols on the perimeter wire.

February, 1920.—On the 23rd February two troops, under Lieutenant Marshall, proceeded to the assistance of Sheikh Ali Shumali. The Sherifean tax enumerator was arrested and his men disarmed and put across the frontier.

March, 1920.—On the 2nd March " B " Squadron, under Captain R. O. Bradley, proceeded to Jisr Mejame and took over posts from the 29th Punjabis, and rejoined on the 8th. From the 10th to the 30th a daily patrol was despatched to

Jisr Mejame and Abu Bassa. On the 28th "C" Squadron marched to Beisan as a patrol of the 36th Jacob's Horse had been attacked near there from the direction of Jisr-ed-Damie. During this period several reports were received from the political authorities that large numbers of Bedouins (400 to 500) were collecting near Kefr Harib on the hills above the camp with a view to attacking the regiment in force; but no attack took place.

April, 1920.—On the 1st April Major E. M. Nixon proceeded on leave and the command devolved on Captain E. W. Spurgin, M.C. During April the regiment left in three trains from Semakh for Ludd, there detraining and marching to Sarona. On arrival at Sarona Major R. J. H. Baddeley, M.C., rejoined and took over command.

October, 1920.—On the 2nd and 7th October the regiment entrained for Kantara and there handed over all horses to Remounts except the few that had been bought out by Officers. Equipment and clothing were replaced by serviceable articles where necessary, and with a few minor exceptions each man was completed with kit and clothing on the same scale as that with which he left India. Of the horses handed over, about one quarter were the original horses brought from India by the regiment in 1914, having been right through the war.

On the 20th October the regiment proceeded to Suez. On the 11th November 1920 the regiment embarked for India, reaching Bolarum on the 25th November.

APPENDIX A

Honours and Awards

Victoria Cross:
Rissaldar Badlu Singh.

Companion of St. Michael and St. George:
Lieutenant-Colonel P. B. Sangster, D.S.O.

Companion of the Order of the Indian Empire:
Major H. R. P. Dickson.

Distinguished Service Order:
Lieutenant-Colonel P. B. Sangster, C.M.G.
    Major W. J. Lambert (and two bars).
    Major F. E. Hunt, O.B.E.
    Captain M. H. Jackson, M.C.
    Captain R. L. W. Herrick.
    Lieutenant J. F. Falconer.

Officer of the British Empire:
Major F. E. Hunt, D.S.O.
Captain A. B. Boggs.

Military Cross:
Major R. J. H. Baddeley.
Captain M. H. Jackson, D.S.O.
    ,,   E. W. Spurgin.
    ,,   R. A. Rice.
    ,,   V. A. Herbert.
    ,,   A. H. H. Armstrong.
    ,,   Haultain (R.A.M.C.).
Lieutenant R. S. King.
    ,,   J. F. Falconer.
Jemadar Jailall Singh.

Legion of Honour :
Major H. Meynell.

Croix de Guerre (French) :
Lance-Duffadar Nur Ali.

Croix de Guerre (Belgian) :
Rissaldar Daya Singh.
Kote-Duffadar Puran Singh.
Duffadar Jailall Singh.

Silver Medal for Military Valour (Italian) :
Lieutenant A. A. Mercer.

Indian Order of Merit :

Jemadar Hayat Ali Beg.
   ,,   Abdul Rahim Khan.
Kote-Duffadar Puran Singh.
Duffadar Jot Ram, I.D.S.M.
Acting Lance-Duffadar Dharam Singh.
Sowar Bhagwan Singh.

Sowar Indar Singh.
  ,,   Chandan Singh.
  ,,   Jitu Singh.
  ,,   Balwant Singh.
  ,,   Hukam Singh.

Order of British India :
Rissaldar-Major and Honorary Lieutenant Chanda Singh.
      ,,   Ghulam Dastagir Khan.
      ,,   Hayat Ali Beg.
      ,,   Ahmed Khan.
Rissaldar Daya Singh.
   ,,   Jaggan Singh.
   ,,   Subh Ram.

Indian Distinguished Service Medal :

Rissaldar Chanda Singh.
   ,,   Kabul Singh.
Woordie-Major Natha Singh.
Jemadar Mohan Singh.
Kote-Duffadar Lall Singh.
    ,,   Imdad Ali.
    ,,   Dale Ram.
    ,,   Pirthi Singh.
Duffadar Daryao Singh.
   ,,   Kasim Ali.
   ,,   Abdul Rahim Khan.
Lance-Duffadar Mohammad Hafiz.
    ,,   Jot Ram.
    ,,   Mir Haider Ali.

Acting Lance-Duffadar Sanwal Singh.
      ,,   Bhima Singh.
Sowar Hira Singh.
  ,,   Ali Mohd. Khan.
  ,,   Karan Singh.
  ,,   Imrat Singh.
  ,,   Mool Singh.
  ,,   Ram Dayal.
  ,,   Ghasi Ram.
  ,,   Ram Chander.
  ,,   Nika Singh.
  ,,   Khem Singh.
  ,,   Ram Chander.

Indian Meritorious Service Medal:

Kote-Duffadar Mangal Singh.
" Molar Singh.
" Bakhtawar Singh.
" Kahan Singh.
" Abdul Rehman Khan.
" Sita Ram.
" Ram Charan Singh.
" Narpat Singh.
Quartermaster-Duffadar Kadir Mohd.
" Jaswant Singh.
" Mohd. Safi.
" Kishan Singh.
Duffadar Nihal Singh.
" Basti Singh.
" Indar Singh.
" Amin Lall.
" Shib Dayal.
" Ghulam Mohd.
" Niaz Mohd.
" Kan Singh.
" Partab Singh.
" Biram Singh.
" Shiam Singh.
" Mangal Singh.
" Karim-ud-Din.
Havildar Habib. Khan.
1st Class S.A.S. Ram Lall.
Lance-Duffadar Feroz Khan.
Lance-Duffadar Shiam Singh.
" Bal Kishan.
" Ram Bilas.
" Mit Singh.
" Ram Lall.
" Palla Singh.
Acting Lance-Duffadar Mohd. Hussein.
" Bhagwant Singh.
Sowar Hafizullah Beg.
" Rattan Singh.
" Sundar Singh.
" Nawab Din.
" Kanwal Singh I.
" Bhagat Singh.
" Wariam Singh.
" Nabi Bux.
" Kharak Singh.
" Sundar Singh.
" Tungal Khan.
" Kanwal Singh II.
" Mendu Singh.
" Jiwan Singh.
" Sundar Singh.
" Lekh Ram.
" Sukh Lall.
" Ram Chander.
Farrier Nihal Singh.

APPENDIX B

British Officers who served on Active Service with the 29th Lancers

1914

Lieutenant-Colonel H. Pollard.
        ,,   A. R. Saunders.
Major Lillingstone.
  ,,   V. K. Birch.
Captain H. Meynell.
   ,,   G. Marchant.
   ,,   G. W. Hemans.
   ,,   Henderson.
   ,,   C. V. Martin.
   ,,   M. H. Jackson.
Lieutenant R. D. Wright.
      ,,   R. O. Bradley.
      ,,   E. W. Spurgin.
      ,,   A. B. Boggs.

1915

4th April	Major W. J. Lambert.
5th ,,	Second-Lieutenant A. A. Mercer (Reserve of Officers).
17th ,,	Major B. Murray White (to 26th January 1916).
17th ,,	Captain C. O. Nicholson (Scottish Horse).
17th ,,	Lieutenant Wedderburn Ogilvy (to 23rd November 1915).
8th July	Second-Lieutenant R. A. Rice (Indian Army Reserve).
31st ,,	Lieutenant H. D. Ash (Volunteer Officer).
1st August	Major R. E. Cheyne (8th Cavalry).
20th ,,	Second-Lieutenant E. N. W. Johnstone (Indian Army Reserve).
30th ,,	Lieutenant J. F. Falconer (Indian Army Reserve).
30th ,,	Second-Lieutenant R. L. W. Herrick (Indian Army Reserve).
30th ,,	Second-Lieutenant D. F. Cunningham Reid (Indian Army Reserve).
20th September	Captain Rennick (11th Lancers).
31st October	Second-Lieutenant J. F. Follit (Indian Army Reserve).
31st ,,	Monsieur De Gloss (Interpreter).

1916

5th February	Second-Lieutenant L. C. Clark (Special Reserve).
5th ,,	Second-Lieutenant J. C. Fitzgibbon (Special Reserve), to 11th April 1916.
11th May	Second-Lieutenant V. A. Herbert (Indian Army Reserve), Adjutant, 26th February 1917 to 8th May 1919.
19th ,,	Second-Lieutenant J. C. J. O'Connor (Indian Army Reserve).
7th August	Major P. B. Sangster (2nd Lancers), Commandant, 7th August 1916.

25th October		Second-Lieutenant H. C. Bell (Indian Army Reserve).
7th December		Lieutenant C. M. Collett (Indian Army Reserve).
7th	,,	Lieutenant E. L. Gavaghan (Indian Army Reserve).
7th	,,	Second-Lieutenant J. C. Williams (Indian Army Reserve) to 12th May 1917.

1917

30th March		Monsieur Le Grain (Interpreter).
5th April		Major R. J. H. Baddeley (15th Lancers).
19th	,,	Second-Lieutenant C. M. O. Sawers (from Base).
8th July		Lieutenant G. D. Baines (33rd Cavalry).
8th	,,	Lieutenant H. F. Halifax (Indian Army Reserve), to 20th July 1917.
10th September		Second-Lieutenant R. S. King (from Base), Adjutant from 8th May 1919.
15th	,,	Second-Lieutenant C. Harvey (from Base).
15th	,,	Second-Lieutenant T. Y. Hawkes (from Base).
18th	,,	Second-Lieutenant A. G. Petrie (from Base).
2nd December		Second-Lieutenant A. E. Cashmore (from Base), to 18th June 1918.

1918

September		Lieutenant E. R. V. Ashton (from Base).
14th November		Lieutenant V. L. Parker (from Base).
29th	,,	Lieutenant P. D. Burch (from Base), to 8th January 1919.
29th	,,	Lieutenant G. F. Jones (7th Lancers).
1st December		Lieutenant C. A. Cairns (from Base).
18th	,,	Lieutenant C. E. Stewart (from Base), to April 1919.
23rd	,,	Lieutenant G. B. Jackson (from Base).

1919

21st March		Lieutenant C. Marshall (31st Lancers).
21st	,,	Lieutenant G. W. B. Jacob (from Base).
13th July		Lieutenant A. P. Leigh (25th Cavalry), to 10th September 1919.
November		Lieutenant W. R. Carr (from Base).
1st December		Major E. M. Nixon (36th Jacob's Horse).

Medical Officers :

Captain Haultain (R.A.M.C.), till 9th May 1918.
   ,,   G. D. Malhoutra (I.M.S.), till November 1918.
   ,,   S. K. Sanyal (I.M.S.), till November 1919.

APPENDIX C

OFFICERS, NON-COMMISSIONED OFFICERS AND MEN OF THE 29TH LANCERS (DECCAN HORSE) WHO LOST THEIR LIVES IN THE WAR

Lieutenant-Colonel C. V. Martin.
Major G. W. Hemans.
  ,,   G. Marchant.
Lieutenant E. R. V. Ashton.
  ,,   J. F. Follit.

Rissaldar-Major Inder Singh.
Rissaldar Badan Singh.
Ressaidar Newal Singh.
  ,,   Badlu Singh.
Jemadar Jahan Singh.
  ,,   Mohd. Umar Khan.
  ,,   Dale Ram Singh.
  ,,   Nihal Singh.
Kote-Duffadar Pirthi Singh.
  ,,   Balwant Singh.
Duffadar Arjan Singh.
  ,,   Shiblal Singh.
  ,,   Govinda Singh.
  ,,   Inder Singh.
  ,,   Raltan Singh.
  ,,   Mehrchand Singh.
  ,,   Nand Lall.
  ,,   Abdul Nabi.
Lance-Duffadar Mam Chand.
  ,,   Bakhtawer Singh.
  ,,   Inder Singh.
  ,,   Najaf Ali.
  ,,   Dalip Singh.
  ,,   Shadi Ram Singh.
  ,,   Lehri Singh.
  ,,   Chainchal Singh.
  ,,   Khazan Singh.
  ,,   Prem Singh.
  ,,   Shadi Ram.
Acting Lance-Duffadar Ralla Singh.
  ,,   Ishar Singh.
  ,,   Ismail-ud-din.
  ,,   Horam Singh.
  ,,   Rahman Khan.
  ,,   Ram Sarup.
  ,,   Rahim Ali Khan.
  ,,   Lall Khan.

Acting Lance-Duffadar Dasonda Singh.
  ,,   Jaimal Singh.
  ,,   Sheo Chand.
  ,,   Mohd. Khan.
Sowar Ram Singh.
  ,,   Yadram Singh.
  ,,   Harsarup Singh.
  ,,   Lakha Singh.
  ,,   Bhoran Singh.
  ,,   Sisram Singh.
  ,,   Nahar Singh.
  ,,   Inder Singh.
  ,,   Kishan Lal Singh.
  ,,   Jhanda Singh.
  ,,   Amar Singh.
  ,,   Bhawar Singh.
  ,,   Nand Singh.
  ,,   Wazir Singh.
  ,,   Mohd. Beg.
  ,,   Sis Ram.
  ,,   Shk. Abdul Wahab.
  ,,   Raghbir Singh I.
  ,,   Kishan Singh.
  ,,   Randhir Singh.
  ,,   Gopal Singh.
  ,,   Zalim Singh.
  ,,   Chandan Singh.
  ,,   Sant Singh.
  ,,   Dayaram Singh.
  ,,   Mukhtiar Singh I.
  ,,   Sisram Singh.
  ,,   Lekhram Singh.
  ,,   Shib Charam.
  ,,   Hoshiar Singh.
  ,,   Kishan Lall Singh.
  ,,   Shib Dayal.
  ,,   Mukhtiyar Singh II.
  ,,   Lakhpat Singh.

Sowar Mukhtiyar Singh III.
," Raghbir Singh II.
," Biram Singh.
," Bhikan Singh.
," Risal Singh.
," Nahar Singh.
," Ram Singh.
," Mool Chand Singh.
," Raghbir Singh III.
," Jahori Singh.
," Ghazi Ram.
," Jagram Singh.
," Dall Singh.
," Abdulla Khan.
," Risal Singh.
," Mukhtiar Singh.
," Nathu Singh.
," Sudhan Singh.
," Randhir Singh.
," Kharak Singh.
," Gafoor Khan.
," Sudhan Singh.
," Umrao Singh.
," Kallu Singh.
," Sheikh Abdul Kadir.
," Ram Lall.
," Chatter Singh.
," Baljit Singh.
," Sheikh Abdul Rahim.
," Siri Chand Singh.
," Thaman Singh.
," Tej Singh.
," Roop Ram.
," Shib Singh.
," Ram Singh.
," Imrat Singh.
," Bhoma Singh.
," Shib Lall.
," Bhoop Singh.
," Lokh Chand.
," Ram Lall.
," Ranjit Singh.
," Netram Singh.
," Daryoo Singh.
," Pirbhoo Singh.
," Nazir Ali.
," Alladad Khan.
," Hari Singh.
," Mool Chand.
," Indar Singh.
," Surat Singh.
," Ram Singh.

Sowar Kamal Singh.
," Mohd. Hussein.
," Raj Singh.
," Leela Singh.
," Fatteh Singh.
," Shk. Abdul Rahman.
," Ram Singh.
," Reoti Lall Singh.
," Harphul Singh.
," Chandghi Ram.
," Bharat Singh.
," Arjan Singh.
," Bikambar Singh.
," Kanak Singh.
," Karan Singh.
," Dal Chand.
," Umrao Singh.
," Hari Singh.
," Sagar Singh.
," Chet Ram.
," Khazan Singh I.
," Shk. Sardari.
," Khazan Singh II.
," Syed Burhan.
," Shanker Singh.
," Nand Singh.
," Kartar Singh.
," Het Ram.
," Bakhshish Singh.
," Jai Dial.
," Mathra Singh.
," Syed Abdul Khadir.
," Abdul Razak.
," Fateh Mohd. Khan.
," Mohd. Ali Khan.
," Hari Lall.
," Gumani Singh.
," Puran Singh.
," Natha Singh.
," Abdul Karim.
Cook Multan Singh.
," Magha.
Ward Orderly Ali Sher Khan.
Mochi Dhan Raj.
," Narain.
," Jai Lal.
Smith Usman Ali.
S.A.S. Nur Mohd.
Tailor Mir Usman Ali.
Mistri Autar.
Syce Muttra.

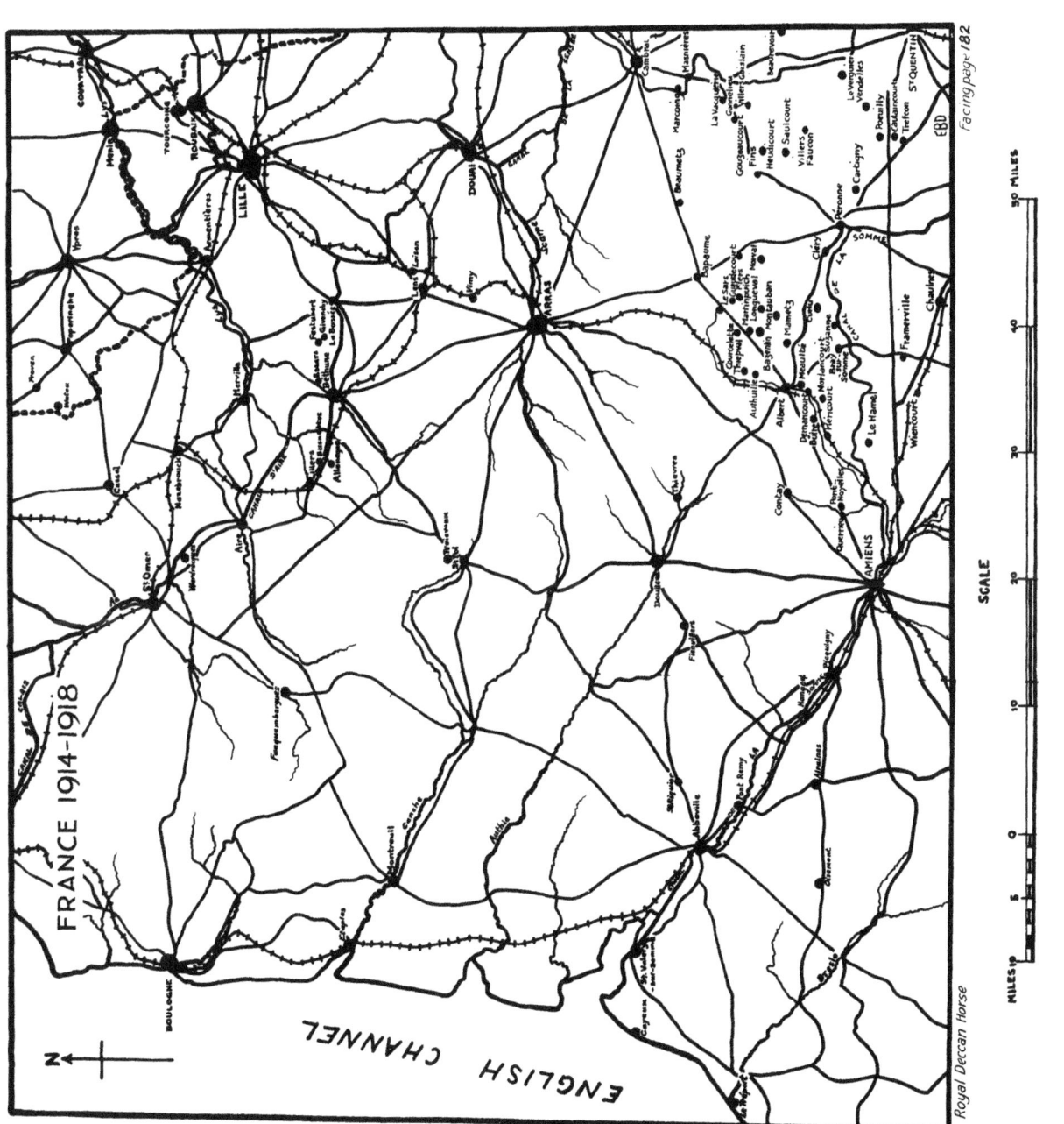

www.ingramcontent.com/pod-product-compliance
Lightning Source LLC
Chambersburg PA
CBHW080549230426
43663CB00015B/2765